A GROUP STUDY OF NINE CRITICAL ISSUES FAC[...]

ISSUES FROM THE EDGE

PERSONAL INTEGRITY

THE ENVIRONMENT

PORNOGRAPHY

WHEN PARENTS ARE SUBSTANCE ABUSERS

LIFE AFTER DEATH

ANTI-SEMITISM

MEDIA VIOLENCE

HOMELESSNESS

PUT-DOWNS

EDITORIAL STAFF

Mark Maddox, Publisher
Gary S. Greig, Ph.D., Senior Editor
Carol Eide, Youth Editor
Darcey M. Baptiste, Editorial Coordinator

CONTRIBUTING EDITORS

Ron Durham, Ph.D.
Judith L. Roth

CONTENTS

ISSUES FROM THE EDGE

This course focuses on nine contemporary issues that are challenging teenagers. Exploring what the Bible says about each of these issues will equip teens to make godly decisions and affect change in their world.

LIFE AFTER DEATH
Ronald Enroth

Focus:
Christians must know what the Bible teaches about the afterlife in order to discern between false beliefs and the truth concerning what happens when a person dies.

Key Verses:
"I am the resurrection and the life. He who believes in me will live, even though he dies; and whoever lives and believes in me will never die." John 11:25,26

THE ENVIRONMENT
Glen Wolfe

Focus:
God has given humankind the responsibility of taking care of the earth.

Key Verses:
"God blessed them and said to them, 'Be fruitful and increase in number; fill the earth and subdue it. Rule over the fish of the sea and the birds of the air and over every living creature that moves on the ground.'...The Lord took the man and put him in the Garden of Eden to work it and take care of it." Genesis 1:28; 2:15

ANTI-SEMITISM
Connie Neal

Focus:
Christians need to respond with compassion to the worldwide tendency to oppress the Jews.

Key Verses:
"I will make you into a great nation and I will bless you; I will make your name great, and you will be a blessing. I will bless those who bless you, and whoever curses you I will curse; and all peoples on earth will be blessed through you." Genesis 12:2,3

MEDIA VIOLENCE
Tom Nash

Focus:
Media violence both reflects and adds to the problem of violence in society. As Christians, we need to learn to appropriately express anger and control our intake of violent media.

Key Verse:
"'In your anger do not sin': Do not let the sun go down while you are still angry." Ephesians 4:26

HOMELESSNESS
Gail Nelsen

Focus:
By sharing God's concern for the needs of the homeless, we are expressing our gratitude for God's love for us.

Key Verse:
"I know that the Lord secures justice for the poor and upholds the cause of the needy." Psalm 140:12

PUT-DOWNS
Tom Finley

Focus:
God wants us to use language that will build others up.

Key Verse:
"Therefore encourage one another and build each other up, just as in fact you are doing." 1 Thessalonians 5:11

INTEGRITY
Dewey Bertolini

Focus:
A commitment to personal integrity among Christians will have a great impact for the cause of Christ in our world.

Key Verses:
"Lord, who may dwell in your sanctuary? Who may live on your holy hill? He whose walk is blameless and who does what is righteous, who speaks the truth from his heart." Psalm 15:1,2

WHEN PARENTS ARE SUBSTANCE ABUSERS
Doug Webster

Focus:
Through the support of the Body of Christ, our heavenly Father provides the person with a substance-abusing parent with the opportunity to be part of a healthy, whole family.

Key Verse:
"My Father, who has given them to me, is greater than all; no one can snatch them out of my Father's hand." John 10:29

PORNOGRAPHY
Connie Neal

Focus:
Repeated exposure to pornography affects a person's perception of sexual intimacy and his or her expectations for relationships.

Key Verses:
"So I tell you this, and insist on it in the Lord, that you must no longer live as the Gentiles do, in the futility of their thinking. They are darkened in their understanding and separated from the life of God because of the ignorance that is in them due to the hardening of their hearts. Having lost all sensitivity, they have given themselves over to sensuality so as to indulge in every kind of impurity, with a continual lust for more." Ephesians 4:17-19

ABOUT THE

DEWEY BERTOLINI

Dewey has been involved in youth work for over 18 years. He received his Masters of Divinity degree from Talbot Seminary in La Mirada, California and is currently working as Professor of Youth Ministry and Bible at the Master's College in Santa Clarita, California. Dewey has authored several books including *Back to the Heart of Youth Work* (Victor Books) and is a popular conference speaker who focuses on the topic of maintaining and restoring personal integrity.

RONALD ENROTH

Dr. Enroth currently serves as Professor of Sociology at Westmont College in Santa Barbara, California. He has spent the last two decades researching and writing on the subject of current religious movements. His written works include, *The Lure of the Cults and New Religions,* (Inter-Varsity Press) and *Evangelizing the Cults* (Servant Publications). Dr. Enroth conducts seminars focusing on the topic of the cults and new religious movements and has discussed this topic on a number of radio and television programs.

TOM FINLEY

Tom is a veteran youth worker, artist, editor and author of countless curriculum, clip art and resource books for Christian youth workers. These publications include: *I Was a Teenage Clip Art Book* (Gospel Light Publications), *Ecclesiastes: Survival in the 21st Century* (Gospel Light Publications), *Good Clean Fun, Vols. 1 and 2* (Zondervan Publishing House) and *The Complete Junior High Bible Study Resource Books #1-#12* (Gospel Light Publications). Tom is currently working as a free-lance writer and artist, suffering for the Lord in his home in Hawaii.

TOM NASH

Dr. Nash currently serves as Associate Professor of the Communication department at Biola University in La Mirada, California. He teaches courses in radio/TV/film production as well as courses in communication. His graduate work was completed at Michigan State University in East Lansing, Michigan.

AUTHORS

CONNIE NEAL

Connie is a free-lance writer, veteran youth worker, homemaker and mother. She received a Bachelor's degree in Communication from Pepperdine University in Malibu, California. Connie has done research and writing for Jewish/Christian organizations in the San Francisco, California area. She has been personally confronted with the destruction pornography can wield and has been involved in the counseling and healing process of the sexual addiction of a loved one.

DOUG WEBSTER

Doug serves as the Director of Public Affairs for the National Institute of Youth Ministry in San Clemente, California. NIYM exists to help young people make positive life decisions by equipping those who work most closely with them. Doug received a Bachelor's degree in Church Ministry and a Master of Divinity degree from Fuller Theological Seminary in Pasadena, California. Doug has also served as a pastor and has been involved in the ministry of New Life Treatment Centers, Inc. New Life is committed to administering Christ-centered care to adolescents and adults in crisis.

GAIL NELSEN

Gail is a social worker involved in the ministry of Project Understanding in Ventura, California. Gail ministers to the needs of homeless and poor families in the Ventura area, providing counseling, education and help with physical and social needs. Project Understanding is a growing, community-based program committed to advocacy and personal care for the poor and homeless.

GLEN WOLFE

Dr. Wolfe is currently serving as Professor of Chemistry at Ventura College in Ventura, California. The courses he teaches include environmental chemistry. He received his Doctorate degree from the University of Arizona in Tuscon, Arizona. He is an active member of his local congregation and enjoys writing, music and time with his family.

How to Use This Course

No one knows your students as well as you do. No one has the grasp of their interest level, needs, maturity and spiritual awareness that you have as their leader. Because of this, you need to be able to create lessons that meet the real needs of your students. These Bible study materials are designed to help you do just that.

This coursebook consists of three parts: the **Teacher's Manual** section, which gives you background information and directions for the Bible study sessions; the **Student Worksheets and Resource Pages** section, which contains the reproducible worksheets and resource materials referred to in the teaching plans; and the **Design-It-Yourself!** section which contains a variety of reproducible pieces for use with your group. Let's take a closer look at these tools and how they can be used.

TEACHER'S MANUAL SECTION

Each session contains a Key Verse, Biblical Basis, Focus, Aims, Teacher's Bible Study and Teaching Plan.

The **Teacher's Bible Study** provides you with the background information you need for presenting the session material.

Each **Teaching Plan** gives you a(n):

Approach—to catch the students' interest in the session topic;

Bible Exploration—to examine Scripture and its meaning for life today;

Conclusion—to guide students in making personal application of the Bible truths presented in the session.

We have created the teaching plans to be flexible. If you have limited time, cut and paste the different activities and options to create a learning experience that fits both your time frame and your students' needs.

STUDENT WORKSHEETS AND RESOURCE PAGES SECTION

This feature allows you to customize the course. These reproducible pages can be used any way you like. You can use them as is or adapt them to your students' needs. The basic intent is to involve your students in searching Scripture, thinking about it, interpreting it and applying it to their personal lives. The worksheets and resource pages can be used two ways.

• **Use Them as Is:** The worksheets and resource pages are designed so you can simply pop them out of the book (they are perforated) and make the necessary number of copies on a photocopy machine. Prepare enough worksheets for your students and a few extra for visitors. Follow the directions in the teaching plans for using the resource pages.

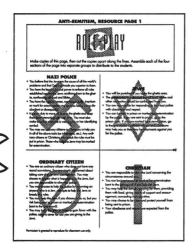

- **Cut Them Up:** They may be customized any way you wish. Cut out portions you will not be using; add relevant Bible verses or questions. Note that the pages are printed on one side only to allow for this. The material is copyrighted, but permission is given for you to use and copy the worksheets and resource pages for use with your students. (This does not apply to the Teacher's Manual section.) Be creative! Use the material selectively, zeroing in on what works best with your students.

DESIGN-IT-YOURSELF! SECTION

In this section you will find several handy tools. The first is a full-page flyer you can complete, photocopy and mail or post to advertise this course. There is also a page that contains two smaller versions of this flyer that can be completed, copied, cut apart and used as bulletin inserts or handouts.

The second item you will find is a reproducible master for a Bible reading chart. Customize this chart to provide your students with the resources for a daily time with God. You may want to use the Key Verse and the Biblical

Basis from each session to design meaningful reading assignments for your students. For each daily reading assignment, include questions based on a portion of the Scripture you have chosen.

The third item is a reproducible master for a letter to parents. By adding appropriate verses and discussion questions to this letter, you can give parents a tool for interacting with their teens on the topics you are studying. Design a separate letter for each session you will be teaching. Make copies of each letter and, as you study each issue, send the corresponding letter to the parents of your students. Doing this will stimulate discussion in the home, reinforce your teaching and support and involve the parents of your teens.

MAKE SOMETHING OF IT

The editors of this course want the time you spend with your students to be spiritually rewarding. Use the material in this coursebook to give you ideas, input and guidance—to spark your thinking and creativity. We pray that the tools in this book will help to make your ministry effective for eternity.

FOR A 13-WEEK TEACHING PLAN

There are nine sessions in this coursebook. If you are teaching on a 13-week quarter system, use the following suggestions to adapt several of the sessions to extend over two weeks.

- During your next meeting after teaching the session on "The Environment" involve your students in a group outing that will reinforce the need to appreciate and care for God's creation. This could include cleaning up around the church building, gathering materials for recycling, visiting a scenic spot and having a time of praise and appreciation for what God has made.

- At the end of your session on "Media Violence" give your students one of the following assignments: (1) For one or two evenings, keep count of the number of TV shows you watch. When watching, keep count of the number of times an act of violence is used to resolve a situation and the number of times a peaceful solution is used to resolve a situation. (2) Count the number of songs on the recordings (records, cassettes, CDs) you personally own. Read through the lyrics of each song on each recording and count the number of songs that support the use of violence against self or another person. Calculate the percentage of the songs you have that support violence compared to the total number of songs in your collection.

During your next meeting after giving these assignments, discuss the students' findings and their feelings about what they have discovered. Have a time of sharing about real-life situations where your students must make decisions about expressing anger appropriately. Resource that can help stimulate discussion in this area include *Outrageous Object Lessons* and *The Youth Worker's Book of Case Studies* (see p. 127 for more information about these and other resources).

- During your next meeting after teaching the session on "Homelessness," arrange for your group to visit a homeless shelter, serve in a soup kitchen or have a representative from an organization that ministers to the needs of the homeless speak to your students.

- After teaching each of the issues in this book, have a time of review and reflection of the topics. Ask students to share insights they have received from the study and any impact discussing these topics has had on their daily life. You may want to keep this time informal and provide refreshments.

About Involvement Learning

So often we hear or read accounts of youth whose lives are empty and they have no apparent goals. To fill the emptiness, they often turn to activities that ultimately only heighten that emptiness. Now more than ever, today's youth need to know that the potential to live a dynamic, meaningful life is firmly rooted in study of and obedience to God's Word.

It takes courage to live an obedient life and it takes strength to overcome the many barriers to Christian growth erected by the world. Therefore, it may not be enough to simply *tell* today's youth that studying and obeying God's Word will lead to a productive life. Many teachers have helped their youth *know* this truth for themselves by *showing* them through involvement learning.

The teaching methods and activities in this book emphasize involvement learning. These methods will take your students from passively listening to actively digging into the Scriptures. These methods will help you create in your students the desire to personally examine God's Word and to make practical applications of the truths being studied.

Each session in this course is composed of three parts and each part serves a specific purpose:

- **Approach**—involves students in activities that capture and direct their interest toward the theme of the session.
- **Bible Exploration**—involves students in a variety of activities to learn what the Bible says about the session's theme.
- **Conclusion**—provides each student with an opportunity to apply the Bible truth to his or her own life.

The ideas provided in these sessions may stimulate additional ideas of your own which are more suitable for your group and teaching style. It is our prayer that the learning experiences suggested in this book, coupled with the power of God's Word, will challenge and motivate your students—encouraging some to become Christians and motivating growth in those who have become complacent in their spiritual lives.

Check How You're Doing

After each session do the following:

1. Review the session aims. Did you help students accomplish the aims? What evidence do you have to indicate the goals were reached? If not, why not? What could have been changed? To what degree are you *sure* students understood the main points?

2. Think about your use of time. Were you able to control the time, or did it slip away from you? Did you give the students enough warning about the time they had to complete their projects? Don't be chained to the clock, but have a timed plan.

3. Consider the appropriateness of the session theme. Were the methods and questions right for your students? There will be times when you should modify your session plans on the spot to accommodate a question which arises. There are even times when you should put aside the entire lesson and deal with a specific problem at hand. Be flexible.

4. Think about the students' participation. Who talked? Who didn't? Did your questions draw out non-talkers? What questions received immediate answers? Which seemed more difficult? How could you have encouraged more participation?

5. How well are you getting to know your students as individuals? What are their interests, needs and problems? What is their level of spiritual growth? What problems are they having? It takes time and planning to find out this kind of information and you need to stay constantly updated. Plan time to make these conversations happen.

Take a moment now and list what you know about your students, what you need to know and what you will do to follow up on their needs.

6. How did the session Scriptures affect you as you taught? Were you personally influenced by the session theme, discussions and activities? Do you think the students sensed your enthusiasm and interest? How could you improve?

7. Pray about the past session and the next session. Share fears, joys, failures and successes with the Lord.

PRESENTING CHRIST TO YOUNG PEOPLE

How do you present Christ to a young person?

1. *Pray.* Ask God to prepare the young person to receive the message and to prepare you to present it.

2. *Lay the foundation.* Youth are evaluating you and the Lord you serve by everything you do and say. They are looking for people in whose lives knowing God makes a noticeable difference, for people who love them and listen to them—the same way God loves them and listens to them.

Learn to listen with your full attention. Learn to share honestly both the joys and the struggles you encounter as a Christian. Be honest about your own questions and about your personal concern for the students. Learn to accept your kids as they are. Christ died for them while they were sinners.

3. *Be aware of opportunities.* A student may ask to talk after class. Or some might be waiting for you to suggest going for a Coke. These are opportunities to get together and share what Jesus Christ means to you.

4. *Have a plan.* Don't lecture or force the issue. Here are some tips to keep in mind:

a. *Put the student at ease.* Be perceptive of feelings and remember that he or she is probably nervous. Be relaxed, natural and casual in your conversation, not critical or judgmental.

b. *Get him or her to talk,* and listen carefully to what is said. Students sometimes make superficial or shocking statements just to get your reaction. Don't begin lecturing or problem-solving. Instead encourage him or her to keep talking.

c. *Be gently direct.* Students may have trouble bringing up the topic. If you sense this, a simple question like, "How are you and God getting along?" can unlock a life-changing conversation.

d. *Discuss God's desire to have fellowship with people.* As you relate the plan God has for enabling people to have a relationship with Him, move through the points slowly enough to allow time for thinking and comprehending. However, do not drag out the presentation. Cover the following points:

- God's goal for us is abundant life (John 3:16; John 10:10).

- All people are separated from God by sin (Rom. 3:23; 6:23).

- God's solution is Jesus Christ who died to pay the penalty for our sin (John 14:6; Rom. 5:8).

- Our response is to receive Christ as Savior (John 1:12).

e. *Make sure the student understands* that accepting Christ is very simple, though very profound. If you feel the student understands, ask if he or she would like to accept Christ now. If so, ask the student to pray with you. Explain that praying is simply talking to God. In this case it's telling God of the student's need for Christ and desire for Christ to be in his or her life as personal Lord and Savior. Then suggest that the student study the Bible in order to begin growing in the faith. Using the study tool, *So, What's a Christian Anyway?* (see p. 127), is a good starting point.

If your young person feels unready to make a decision, suggest Scriptures to read and make an appointment to get together again. John 14—16, Romans 3—8 and the Gospel of Mark are good sections to suggest for reading. In the meantime, pray for the student.

5. *Remember* your responsibility is simply to present the gospel and to be able to explain the hope that is within you. It is the Holy Spirit who makes a person's heart ready for a relationship with God and gives growth.

WHEN IT'S ALL SAID AND DONE (FOLLOW-UP)

When it's all said and done, what is done will far outlast what is said.

The time you invest in building relationships, encouraging and affirming students, listening to them and putting up with their rowdy moods (which seem to be never ending) will pay dividends in the Kingdom of God.

It is the personal touch that does it. Kids know when someone cares for them. It shows. It declares loudly, "Here is a real person who has a real relationship with Christ, and who wants to know the real me."

Relationships should not end with the packing away of materials. New contacts have been made during these days. These contacts need to be followed up.

Plan follow-up for those students who become Christians. Get them into a regular Bible study. Visit their homes to answer questions and give encouragement. Provide transportation to youth group events when needed.

Plan follow-up for those who rededicate their lives to the Lord. They need guidance in Bible study, in prayer and in preparing for the work the Lord has for them.

Plan follow-up for the unsaved. Invite them to youth group activities. Bring them to your Bible studies and worship services. Continue to pray for them by name and keep in touch with them. Remember birthdays with a card or phone call.

Plan follow-up for unchurched parents. Show genuine interest in their young people. Continue to invite the entire family to church services and to adult Bible classes.

And when the once ornery kid begins to respond to the love and caring you have shown, don't be surprised if he or she thinks about your demonstration of God's love—and then tries to do the same for someone else.

LIFE AFTER DEATH

RONALD ENROTH

KEY VERSES

"I am the resurrection and the life. He who believes in me will live, even though he dies; and whoever lives and believes in me will never die." John 11:25,26

BIBLICAL BASIS

Matthew 25:41; Luke 16:23-26; 23:43; John 14:1-3; 2 Thessalonians 1:8-10; Hebrews 3:19; 9:27; 1 Peter 1:3,4; 2 Peter 3:8-15; Revelation 7:15-17; 14:9-13; 21:3,4,23-27

FOCUS OF THE SESSION

Christians must know what the Bible teaches about the afterlife in order to discern between false beliefs and the truth concerning what happens when a person dies.

AIMS OF THIS SESSION

You and your students will have accomplished the purpose of this Bible study session if you can:

- EXAMINE how cults and false religions view death and the afterlife;
- COMPARE non-Christian beliefs to what the Bible says about death and the afterlife and DISCUSS why it is important for Christians to know what the Bible teaches about life after death;
- CONSIDER the impact personal beliefs about death and the afterlife have on your future and PRAY to accept Christ as the Holy Spirit leads.

TEACHER'S BIBLE STUDY

It has been said that one can never look directly at the sun or at one's own death. Yet the topics of death and the afterlife have both fascinated and frightened people since the beginning of recorded history. Regardless of cultural boundaries or social class, men and women have speculated about the life after death. "If a man dies, will he live again?" was Job's timeless question (Job 14:14). Do we survive the physical experience we call death?

Belief in some form of life after death is nearly universal. The ancient Egyptians placed various items in the tombs of their loved ones and rulers in the hope that these objects would prove useful in the next world. Primitive tribes have conceived of heaven in locations such as the center of the earth, an island paradise or a shadowy spirit realm just beyond the sight of humans. Nordic people spoke of Valhalla; Eastern religionists hope for Nirvana, a "heavenly" state which can be partially realized in this life by the "enlightened."

Studies have shown, not surprisingly, that religion does shape assumptions that we have about the afterlife. And, of course, concepts about life after death shape beliefs and behavior in this life. Survey research has revealed that more than 70 percent of the population 18 years of age and older believe in some form of life after death.[1]

In this session, we will explore some of the beliefs that

cults and nontraditional religions hold regarding death and life after death. We will then compare those beliefs to the perspective of biblical faith. By demonstrating the variety of beliefs people hold concerning the afterlife, we can equip our students to discern truth from error.

Cultic Views

The belief systems of cults and new religious movements are in conflict with biblical faith at many points, not just in regards to life after death. While it is not possible to summarize here the major doctrines and practices of cultic groups, a brief review of their teachings about death and the afterlife will point to their deficient theology in other areas such as salvation, the nature of God, sin and the role of Jesus Christ.

Mormons. The Mormon Church (Latter-Day Saints) subscribes to the notion of eternal progression—that we are in the process of learning how to become gods.[2] Mormon men expect to become gods in the afterlife, with their own planet to rule over and to populate.[3] Mormons believe in universal salvation; that all people will eventually be saved.[4]

Mormonism also teaches the bodily resurrection of all men and women to one of three heavens: the telestial, the terrestrial and the celestial.[5] The telestial heaven is for heathen people who reject the gospel (the Mormon gospel). The terrestrial or second heaven will be for Christians who did not accept Mormonism and for people of good will of other religions. The celestial heaven is reserved for Mormons and is divided into three levels. Special celestial status is accorded those Mormons whose marriage was eternally sealed in a Mormon temple while here on earth.

Jehovah's Witnesses. The Watchtower Bible and Tract Society (better known as Jehovah's Witnesses) teaches that the human soul is not eternal, but mortal, and that it can die.[6] Even Jesus, according to their view, did not have an immortal soul.[7] Animals, they claim, have souls as humans do and only misguided "religionists" believe otherwise. When the human body dies, the soul ceases to exist. It cannot be materially separated from the body. The same is true for an animal.

Witnesses also believe that the spirit is distinct from the soul and is unique to humans (as opposed to animals). When a person dies, Jehovah takes back the spirit. The soul—the part of the person that exists in a conscious

state—ceases to exist. At the time of resurrection the spirit is returned by Jehovah and a new body is constituted.

Jehovah's Witnesses teach that heaven (the Kingdom of Jehovah) will be limited to 144,000 faithful followers (a misinterpretation of Rev. 7:4).[8] The 144,000 elect will rule with King Jesus while the remaining faithful Witnesses will spend eternity on paradise earth. All others will be annihilated.

Witnesses reject any notion of hell in terms of eternal punishment.[9] They teach that any doctrine of hell is unreasonable, unscriptural and contrary to God's love and justice. Hell is a doctrine contrived by an "organized religion," of "hell fire screechers."[10] *The Watchtower* interprets hell, or sheol, as the grave, a place of extinction or annihilation.

Christian Scientists. The followers of the Christian Science religion deny all physical existence.[11] It is a religion of mind over matter, and health is a primary focus of their devotion. To the Christian Scientist, the physical world is "an illusion of mortal mind."[12] The material world has no reality, only the mind or spirit is real. Therefore, according to Christian Science teaching, death is an illusion; there can be no death, for death is unreal; it is the opposite of good, of God.[13] The word "death" was banned for years from the *Christian Science Monitor,* the newspaper owned and controlled by the Christian Science Church.

According to Christian Scientists, an afterlife in heaven is not possible since heaven, as an actual place, does not exist. Heaven is a divine state of mind; heaven is harmony, boundless bliss.[14] In her book, *Science and Health with Key to the Scriptures,* founder Mary Baker Eddy wrote: "The sinner makes his own hell by doing evil, and the saint his own heaven by doing right."[15]

Scientologists. Members of the Church of Scientology promote the writings of their founder, L. Ron Hubbard, which are heavily influenced by Eastern/occult thinking. Although Scientologists claim that their beliefs do not conflict with other religions, there are many instances in which Scientology and biblical faith *do* conflict. For example, Mr. Hubbard has mocked the biblical doctrine of heaven and denied the existence of hell. Scientologists believe in the existence of past lives and argue that many problems besetting the human race may be traced back to these past experiences.

> By demonstrating the variety of beliefs people hold concerning the afterlife, we can equip our students to discern truth from error.

Adherents of Unity. The Unity School of Christianity (also known simply as Unity) was founded in the late nineteenth century and continues to be a very popular religious movement. Like other cults, Unity uses biblical language to promote its non-Christian teachings.

Unity denies the existence of a literal heaven or hell, claiming that whatever heaven or hell there is can be found only here on earth. Followers of Unity do not subscribe to the biblical teaching of eternal life. The founder of Unity, Charles Fillmore, felt that expecting to experience eternal life after we die is a delusion.[16] Unity, in fact, teaches that by pursuing resurrection here on earth one can achieve perfection of the body. This is related to Unity's interpretation of Jesus' resurrection. They teach that Jesus raised His own body both physically and spiritually and that He is still somewhere on earth in spirit form. Unity also teaches a form of reincarnation.[17]

New Agers and Reincarnationists. The New Age movement is a large assortment of individuals and organizations based essentially on the ideas of Eastern religions, including reincarnation. Eastern cults and other reincarnationists believe that the soul experiences multiple lives, gradually achieving a state of perfection and merging with (being absorbed into) the Universal Soul, the Cosmos or god.

Reincarnation is a very old belief. The influence of reincarnation in the Western world continues to grow at a rapid rate. A 1982 Gallup Poll revealed that 23 percent of the United States' population believe in some form of reincarnation.[18] Many people are convinced that "afterlife experiences" prove life after death and make the possibility of reincarnation something to be seriously considered.

Biblical Perspectives

It is important to use biblical language carefully in presenting Scripture's perspective on life after death, and in defending it against the cults. Some Christians have argued against the false doctrine that the soul is annihilated at death by asserting that it is "immortal" in the divine sense taught in ancient Greek philosophy.[19] A definition of terms will help clarify what the Bible teaches.

"Immortality" is the quality of divine life that distinguishes it from mortal, or perishable, life. In this sense, only God is *inherently* immortal (see 1 Tim. 6:15,16).

It is not human nature, but the the gospel, that makes immortality available to us (see 2 Tim. 1:10). God promises to "clothe" the saved with this quality of life at the resurrection (see 1 Cor. 15:53-55).

"Death" and "perish" as used in the Bible do not imply annihilation, but separation. Physical death is the separation of the body from the spirit. Spiritual death is separation from God. Hell, or eternal death, is the state of being eternally separated from God just as heaven, or eternal life, is dwelling with God eternally. Neither implies the cessation of existence.

"Existence after death" is a quality of life shared by everyone, believer and unbeliever alike. Jesus taught that people may kill the body but they cannot kill the soul (see Matt. 10:28). Christians have always believed that the soul lives on after the death of the body. We are only tenants, temporarily occupying a physical, earthly body (see 2 Cor. 4:16; 5:8; 1 Tim. 6:7,8). The distinction between body and soul (also referred to as the spirit) is demonstrated in both the Old Testament (see Job 32:8,18; Isa. 57:16; Zech 12:1) and the New Testament (see Acts 7:59; 1 Cor. 2:11; Jas 2:26).

Christians assert that an individual's beliefs and actions in this earthly life have implications and consequences for the afterlife. Our Lord's account of the rich man and Lazarus makes this point very effectively (see Luke 16:19-31). Christians believe in a future life because of God's promises revealed in Scripture, because of God's moral character and because of God's justice and righteousness. Justice demands an eternal heaven, but justice is not real without the provision of eternal punishment.

The consequences resulting from a person's beliefs and actions are inevitable. This is illustrated by the words of the apostle Paul as he foresaw the day of God's wrath when He "will give to each person according to what he has done" (Rom. 2:6). The righteous, or those who reject evil and do good, will receive "glory, honor and peace" (v. 10). The flip side of the rewards individuals will receive some day is the dispensing of punishment to those who "reject the truth and follow evil" (v. 8). The unrighteous, or sinners, shall perish (v. 12)—not in the sense of ceasing to exist, but of being eternally banished from God's presence. In terms of life after death, the Christian believes that the destination of every individual will be either

> **Like other cults, Unity uses biblical language to promote its non-Christian teachings.**

eternal heaven or eternal hell. This destination hinges on whether or not the individual is a member of God's family (see Matt. 25:31-46 and Phil. 3:17-21).

A central theme of Christianity is that death is not the end. And the cornerstone of the Christian faith is the resurrection of Jesus Christ. First Corinthians 15 is commonly referred to as the resurrection chapter. Here Paul has emphatically stressed the importance of the resurrection of Christ: "And if Christ has not been raised, our preaching is useless and so is your faith" (v. 14). An individual's future in heaven after death is dependent upon this resurrection. As John 11:25,26 says, "I am the resurrection and the life. He who believes in me will live, even though he dies; and whoever lives and believes in me will never die."

Jesus told His disciples: "In my Father's house are many rooms....I am going there to prepare a place for you" (John 14:2). Jesus promises His followers that one day they will follow Him to the Father's house in heaven. What a fantastic promise! Jesus has assured His followers of advance reservations and has personally gone before us to prepare our rooms.

In 1 Corinthians 15:35-44, Paul speaks of only two forms our bodies will take: the natural and the spiritual. The natural, earthly body has qualities we are all familiar with: perishable, dishonor and weakness. The spiritual, or resurrected, body is characterized by imperishability, glory and power (see vv. 42-44). The spiritual body is a body of flesh and bone which will no longer be restricted by natural limitations (e.g. the resurrection body of Christ—see Luke 24:36-39).

Reincarnation is a myth. We do not have many natural bodies before our final resurrection. The book of Hebrews tells us plainly, "man is destined to die once, and after that to face judgment" (9:27). There is no hint of an opportunity for "getting it right" the second time around. Remember what Jesus said to the thief on the cross next to Him: "I tell you the truth, today you will be with me in paradise" (Luke 23:43). The key word is *today*. Jesus does not promise a reunion in the indefinite future or after a series of reincarnations.

What is heaven like? The Bible doesn't tell us everything about heaven, or the New Jerusalem, but in Revelation 21 and 22 we are given some pretty good clues. We know that death or illness will not be present in heaven. Darkness will be banished forever.

Failure and defeat will be unknown. Heaven will be alive with people. Most important of all, heaven means being in the presence of Christ—eternally. This is the culmination of the gospel, the good news. This is the Christian hope: "Now if we died with Christ, we believe that we will also live with him" (Rom. 6:8).

Notes

1. Michael C. Kearl, *Endings: A Sociology of Death and Dying* (New York: Oxford University Press, 1989), p. 184.
2. Joseph Smith, *Doctrine and Covenants of the Church of Jesus Christ of Latter-Day Saints* (Salt Lake City: Deseret Book Co., 1961), section 76:58 and commentary.
3. Smith, *Doctrine and Covenants*, section 132:19, 20 and commentary; Joseph F. Smith, *Teachings of the Prophet Joseph Smith* (Salt Lake City: Deseret Book Co., 1972), pp. 345, 346.
4. Brigham Young, *Journal of Discourses*, Vol. 3, and Vol. 4 (Liverpool: Orson Pratt, 1856, 1857).
5. Smith, *Doctrine and Covenants*, section 76; B.H. Roberts, *History of the Church*, Vol. 1 (Salt Lake City: Deseret Book Co., 1974), p. 283.
6. *Let God Be True* (Brooklyn: Watchtower Bible and Tract Society, 1952), pp. 59-61.
7. Ibid., p. 63.
8. Ibid., pp. 121, 123, 124.
9. Ibid., pp. 79, 80.
10. Walter Martin, *The Kingdom of the Cults* (Minneapolis: Bethany Fellowship, Inc., 1977), p. 89.
11. Mary Baker Eddy, *Science and Health with Key to the Scriptures* (Boston: First Church of Christ Scientist, 1875), p. 468.
12. Martin, p. 124.
13. Eddy, *Science and Health with Key to the Scriptures* (1875), p. 575.
14. Mary Baker Eddy, *First Church of Christ, Scientist, and Miscellany*, (Boston: First Church of Christ Scientist, 1982), p. 267.
15. Mary Baker Eddy, *Science and Health with Key to the Scriptures* (Boston: First Church of Christ Scientist, 1914), p. 266.
16. Charles Fillmore, *Unity* (Unity Village, MO: Unity School of Christianity, May 1927).
17. *Unity Statement of Faith* (Unity Village, MO: Unity School of Christianity), article 22.
18. *Princeton Religion Research Center Fact Sheet* (Princeton, NJ: Princeton Religion Research Center, Inc., 1982), vol. 4, no. 7.
19. Sinclair B. Ferguson and David F. Wright, eds., *New Dictionary of Theology* (Downers Grove, IL: InterVarsity Press, 1988), pp. 332, 333.

> **A central theme of Christianity is that death is not the end. And the cornerstone of the Christian faith is the resurrection of Jesus Christ.**

TEACHING PLAN

APPROACH (5-10 minutes)

Introduce this session by saying something like this: **Many people don't like talking about death and life after death. It may make them uncomfortable, bring back bad memories, be a boring, depressing topic or even seem a bit spooky. When you're young, death and the afterlife may seem far off, distant. It's often the last thing we want to talk about. But if we are honest with ourselves, it *is* something we at least think about occasionally. Today we are going to take a closer look at death and what happens after a person dies.**

Ask your students how many of them know (or at least remember) their grandparents. Most of them will raise their hands indicating a "yes" response. Ask the same question about their great-grandparents and again request a show of hands. Then ask the same question about their great-great-grandparents and note the obvious results. Then mention the fact that 100 years from now (surely 125 years from now) no one will have a personal memory of their existence. Ask, **What does this fact tell you about the relationship between life and death?** The purpose of this question is to demonstrate the transitory nature of life and the fact that each of us will eventually die. Then ask, **How does a person's view of what happens when he or she dies affect that person's life and actions?**

Move to the Bible Exploration by saying, **Death really is a part of life. Today we are going to look at the different beliefs people have about death and life after death and compare them to what the Bible says.**

ALTERNATE APPROACH (5-10 minutes)

Begin by asking the students why death is often a taboo topic in our society. Then discuss the various ways people in our culture today deny, avoid or camouflage death and dying.

Move to the Bible Exploration by saying something like this: **The Bible is very bold in talking about death and the afterlife. Today we are going to look at the different beliefs people have about death and life after death and compare them to what the Bible says.**

BIBLE EXPLORATION (35-50 minutes)

Materials needed: Bibles, a copy for each student of the "Images of Heaven and Hell" student worksheet, pencils, chalkboard and chalk or newsprint and felt pen.

Preparation: Optional—before this session, arrange to have six people assist you in a short drama presentation. Assign one of the following roles—Mormon, Jehovah's Witness, Christian Scientist, Scientologist, Adherent of Unity, New Ager/Reincarnationist—to each of your volunteers and provide each one with a copy of the "Cultic Views" section of the Teacher's Bible study (permission is granted to reproduce this section of the Bible Study for use in this session only). Prepare the skit as given in the Alternate Step 1 and ask each person to be prepared to answer for his or her role the question, "What happens when a person dies?"

Step 1 (5-10 minutes)

Ask, **What are some different ideas you have heard concerning what happens when a person dies?** List

students' responses on the chalkboard or newsprint. Using information from the Teacher's Bible Study section titled "Cultic Views," share information about how various cults and new religious movements view the topic of death and the afterlife. You may want to list on the chalkboard or newsprint the names and views of the different groups described in this section.

Impress upon your students the fact that we live in a society which offers a spiritual smorgasbord. They are likely to meet people with beliefs and perspectives of death and the afterlife that are very different from what the Bible teaches. You might ask the students to share any experiences they have had discussing the topic of death with people who have non-Christian perspectives.

Move to Step 2 by saying, **Let's compare these beliefs about death and the afterlife with what the Bible teaches.**

Alternate Step 1 (10-12 minutes)

Use this alternate step instead of Step 1 above if you want to incorporate drama in this session (see the Preparation for more information). Set up a "person-on-the-street" interview. Have the visitors you have arranged to be present act as if they are waiting at a bus stop. One at a time, interview each person by asking the following question: "What happens when a person dies?" Allow no more than one minute for each person to respond. After each person has shared, the group acts as if the bus has arrived, they "climb aboard" and move as a group out of the room.

After the group has left, gain the attention of the class and ask, **What are some of the different ideas these people expressed about what happens when a person dies?** As necessary, share information from the Teacher's Bible Study section titled "Cultic Views." You may want to list on the chalkboard or newsprint the names and views of the different groups described in this section.

Impress upon your students the fact that we live in a society which is a spiritual smorgasbord. They are likely to meet people with beliefs and perspectives of death and the afterlife that are very different from what the Bible teaches. You might ask the students to share any experiences they have had discussing the topic of death with people who have non-Christian perspectives.

Move to Step 2 by saying, **Let's compare these beliefs about death and the afterlife with what the Bible teaches.**

Step 2 (15-20 minutes)

Move students into groups of three to six. Distribute pencils and copies of the "Images of Heaven and Hell" student worksheet to each student. Assign each group at least three of the passages listed on the worksheet, making sure that all of the passages have been assigned to a group. Direct the groups to locate in their Bibles and read their assigned Scriptures, then write down what their Scriptures say about heaven or hell. Allow eight to ten minutes for the groups to work, then allow time for sharing about each of the passages on the page.

Ask, **How does what the Bible says about the afterlife differ from the beliefs we looked at earlier?** If you listed the groups and beliefs described in the "Cultic Views" section of the Teacher's Bible Study, refer the students to this list (see Step 1 or the Alternate Step 1).

Step 3 (7-10 minutes)

Discuss the following questions: "Why is it easier for people to believe in heaven than in hell?" "How can we reconcile the idea of eternal punishment and hell with the notion of a loving God?" (Refer to 2 Pet. 3:8-15.) "In what ways do you think heavenly life will be different from earthly life?"

Reaffirm the fact that the Bible tells us that everyone continues to exist after death—whether in heaven or hell (as necessary, refer to Job 19:26,27; Matt. 25:31-46; Rom. 6:5-10; 2 Cor. 5:1-10; Heb. 9:27). Emphasize also that there is no hint in the Bible of nonexistence, annihilation, soul sleep or reincarnation (read aloud Luke 23:43 and Heb. 9:27). Mention that these verses imply that a person does not get a second chance to obey God after he or she dies.

Why do you think it is important to trust what the Bible says rather than the beliefs of non-Christian religions or cults? It is important to emphasize the trustworthiness of the Bible and why it is our authority. Point out that false religions (cults) base their beliefs on sources other than the Bible (like the *Book of Mormon*) or on misinterpretations or distortions of Scripture. For Christians to grow in their relationships with God and share their faith with non-Christians, it is important that we know what the Bible *does* and *does not* say about life after death.

Step 4 (8-10 minutes)

Emphasize to students that while God has not given us all the details about what the afterlife (heaven or hell) will be like, the Bible does provide a window into eternal existence—especially what heaven is like. Optional—read the description of God's heavenly city, the New Jerusalem, as recorded in Revelation 21:3,4,11, 18-27.

Then read aloud John 14:1-3. Ask, **What does Jesus promise in these verses? Why is it important to know what will happen when a person dies? How can this knowledge affect a person's decisions and actions today?** Allow five to eight minutes for discussion.

Move to the Conclusion by saying, **It is important that we accurately understand what happens when we die and that we don't follow false beliefs. The consequences of our beliefs today will be eternal. Let's take a few minutes to review what God says will determine whether or not a person will spend eternity in heaven.**

CONCLUSION (5-8 minutes)

Materials needed: Bibles, chalkboard and chalk or newsprint and felt pen. Optional—copies of the booklet, *So, What's a Christian Anyway?* published by Gospel Light Publications (see p. 127, or a tract outlining the steps involved in becoming a Christian).

Remind students that it is not fashionable in our culture to talk about final judgment. Yet the Bible says that there are only two ways of dying. We can die with faith in Christ, or we can die in our sins. Unbelief can keep us out of heaven. Read aloud Hebrews 3:19.

Work with the students to briefly outline the steps involved in becoming a child of God. Include the following in your list: recognizing that every person has sinned and that it is sin that separates us from God and prevents us from spending eternity in heaven (see Isa. 59:2; Rom. 3:23); understanding that because God loves us, He sent His only Son, Jesus, to die on the cross so that our sins can be forgiven (see John 3:16,17); admitting our sins to God and receiving Jesus as our Savior (see John 1:12; Acts 3:19).

Then allow a time of silence for students to consider what they believe about life after death, and how their beliefs line up with what they have learned the Bible says. Close in prayer, thanking God that He cares so much about us to provide us with the opportunity to spend eternity in heaven in His presence.

Be available after class to talk with any students who express interest in talking more about life after death and becoming a member of God's family. Refer to the article "Presenting Christ to Young People" on p. 12 for more information.

Optional—refer to the "How to Become a Christian" section of the booklet, *So, What's a Christian Anyway?* (or an evangelism tract) for help in presenting Christ to a student.

ANTI-SEMITISM

CONNIE NEAL

KEY VERSES

"I will make you into a great nation and I will bless you; I will make your name great, and you will be a blessing. I will bless those who bless you, and whoever curses you I will curse; and all peoples on earth will be blessed through you." Genesis 12:2,3

BIBLICAL BASIS

Genesis 12:1-3,7; 13:15,16; 15:18; 17:7,8,11,13; 2 Samuel 17:11-16; Psalm 89:20,28-37; Jeremiah 31:31,33-35,37; Ezekiel 37:21,23; Romans 10:12,13; 11:28,29; 2 Corinthians 1:3,4; Hebrews 6:13-18

FOCUS OF THE SESSION

Christians need to respond with compassion to the worldwide tendency to oppress the Jews.

AIMS OF THIS SESSION

You and your students will have accomplished the purpose of this Bible study session if you can:

- EXAMINE four key covenants God made with the Jews and the nation of Israel and DISCUSS their enduring nature;
- LIST reasons why people often oppress the Jews;
- CHOOSE one way you can take heed of Genesis 12:3 and bless the Jews by responding to expressions of anti-Semitism.

TEACHER'S BIBLE STUDY

There is a battle going on for the hearts and minds of youth today. As youth workers, one of our goals is to help our students apply biblical knowledge to the way they think and live—including the way they treat others. Unfortunately, we are not the only ones who are seeking to influence their thinking and behavior. George Dietz, who operates a computer bulletin board and is one of the largest distributors of neo-Nazi literature in America says, "'All I want to do is get the thinking processes going....I'm not interested in reaching old people whose minds are set in concrete.' Dietz estimated that 90 percent of those using his bulletin board are children or young adults."[1]

Anti-Semitism is an issue of increasing influence in today's youth culture. Although the Semitic people include all descendants of Shem—including Arabs—we will use the term "Semite" in reference to the Jews, since they are the common target of anti-Semitic beliefs and actions.

A resurgence of anti-Semitic violence is being seen in the growing popularity of the youth subculture known as Skinheads. These gangs, which involve approximately 2,000 to 5,000 members nationwide, are known for racially motivated acts of violence, anti-Semitic vandalism and the espousing of neo-Nazi beliefs.[2] They recruit youth from teen night spots and use racist rock and roll music as a tool to propagate their beliefs. One Skinhead punk rock group is known as The Final Solution, referring to Hitler's plan to exterminate all Jews.

Greg Winthrow was a former leader in the Skinhead movement. When he announced his separation from the movement, his former gang members attacked him, slit his throat and crucified him. After surviving this brutal attack, he committed himself to warning youth against this neo-Nazi/anti-Semitic hate movement. In profiling the people involved in the Skinheads, Winthrow said: "It's not like their members are a bunch of bitter, decrepit old bigots. They are young people throwing their entire futures into something that is empty....They are the future generation of tomorrow.[3]

John Metzger, a 20-year-old neo-Nazi youth leader who prides himself on organizing these lost young people, said: "We're filling a void in their lives."[4] We can help our students protect themselves from such destructive influences by addressing this issue and helping them form a biblically-sound stance on the issue of anti-Semitism.

The Biblical Basis for Judeo-Christianity

The roots of Christianity are planted deeply and firmly in Jewish soil. The New Testament clearly documents that Jesus was a Jew (see Jesus' genealogy in Matt. 1:2-16; see also Rom. 9:5), as were the twelve disciples and most of the early Church (see Acts 15:5-9; Rom. 11:1,2,11,17,18).

Beyond this, Scripture teaches that in Old Testament days God chose to reveal Himself to the human race by means of a chosen nation, Israel (see 1 Chron. 17:20-22). It was through His relationship with the Jewish nation of Israel that God displayed His power, imparted His law, sent His prophets, gave us His laws and ultimately sent His only begotten Son as the promised Messiah. Jesus said, "salvation is from the Jews" (John 4:22).

God has gone on record before the entire world in giving unconditional and irrevocable promises, or covenants, to the nation of Israel and the Jewish people. Gentile believers are sometimes included in the fulfillment of some of these covenants (see Rom. 11:1,17-27; Gal. 3:7-9; 6:16; Eph. 2:11-13), but we will focus on the special relationship between God and the Jews that these covenants represent. These four key covenants are: the Abrahamic (see Gen. 12:2,3); the Palestinian (see Gen. 13:14-17—note the use of the word "forever" in describ-

ing the terms of the covenant); the Davidic (see 2 Sam. 7:11-16); and the New Covenant (see Jer. 31:31-34; see also Heb. 8:7-13).

Each of these covenants is essential to both the study of anti-Semitism as well as developing a balanced view of our Christian heritage. One crucial thing to note in the study of these covenants is that God did not qualify His maintenance of the promises by the behavior of the nation. In fact, the book of Hosea dramatically demonstrates that, although God would severely discipline Israel, He would never give them up. Since the belief that these covenants have been assigned to some group other than the Jews is a pivotal basis for much anti-Semitic thought, our central focus will be to study the enduring nature of these promises to the Jews and the nation of Israel.

The Bible does show that, because the Jews were given a greater direct revelation of God and His holy law, they were to be an example to the nations and therefore subject to stricter judgment and divine discipline (see Amos 3:2; Luke 12:47,48; Rom. 2:9,10). In Deuteronomy 28:15-68 Moses warned that if the Jews failed to obey God's law, horrendous curses unlike those experienced by any other group of people would come upon them.

A resurgence of anti-Semitic violence is being seen in the growing popularity of the youth subculture known as Skinheads.

The Bible also shows that since the Jews are the chosen people of God, they will become the object of satanic attack. (The imagery of Gen. 37:9,10 suggests that the woman of Rev. 12:1-6,13-17 represents Israel; see also Isa. 66:7-11; Micah 4:10; 5:3.) History has born this out. One of the most fascinating examples of satanic influence upon anti-Semitism comes from studying the development of Adolf Hitler's racial theories. These beliefs led directly to the holocaust in which six million Jews were exterminated in Hitler's attempt to destroy every person of Jewish descent (added to this bloodbath were many others of "non-Aryan" descent and those who sympathized with these oppressed people).

Hitler's racial beliefs can be traced to the writings of Houston S. Chamberlain, particularly his work entitled *Foundations of the Nineteenth Century*. William L. Shirer's book, *The Rise and Fall of the Third Reich*, states clearly that the true source of Chamberlain's anti-Semitic teachings was demonic.

Chamberlain was given to seeing demons who, by his own account, drove him on relentlessly to seek new fields of study and get on with his prodigious writings....Once, in 1896, when he was returning from Italy, the presence of a demon became so forceful that he got off the train at Gardone, shut himself up in a hotel room for eight days and...wrote feverishly on a biological thesis until he had the germ of the theme that would dominate all of his later works: race and history....Since he felt himself goaded on by demons, his books (on Wagner, Goethe, Kant, Christianity and race) were written in the grip of a terrible fever, a veritable trance, a state of self-induced intoxication, so that as he says in his autobiography, *Lebenswege*, he was often unable to recognize them as his own work.[5]

Chamberlain's opposition to Scripture is seen in this statement: "Whoever claimed that Jesus was a Jew was either being stupid or telling a lie....Jesus was not a Jew."[6] This man, driven and inspired by demons, was seen as the spiritual founder of the Nazi party and they "hailed his *Foundations* as the 'gospel of the Nazi movement.'"[7] When he went to his grave on January 11, 1927, Chamberlain held high hopes that all he had preached and prophesied would yet come true under the divine guidance of the new German Messiah [Hitler].[8] Hitler did not disappoint Chamberlain's dying hopes.

The belief that these covenants have been assigned to some group other than the Jews is a pivotal basis for much anti-Semitic thought.

The holocaust was part of a long history of oppression of the Jews testified to in biblical and post-biblical history. The Bible helps us understand these past tribulations experienced by the Jews and the nation of Israel, but it also speaks of a future time of incredible suffering which will come upon Israel (and will include Gentile believers in Jesus Christ). It is important to note that all the great passages which may reflect past events as well as these future events also promise deliverance from this oppression as the final curtain falls. These passages, worthy of further study, include Jeremiah 30 and 31, Daniel 12 (see also Zechariah 13:8,9), Matthew 23:37—24:35 and Romans 11.

Persecution of the Jews seems to stem from a last-ditch effort on the part of Satan to destroy the chosen people (see Rev. 12:1-17) and the refining fire of God's judgment, sent to develop an attitude of repentance and receptivity for the coming of their Messiah, Jesus Christ (see Zech. 13:7—14:21). This final restoration and fulfillment of all the promises God has made to Israel will demonstrate God's righteousness and His amazing grace.

The History of Anti-Semitism

From the earliest sources of recorded history, both secular and Christian anti-Semitism has been a unique phenomenon, going beyond mere racism. "Hatred of the Jew has been humanity's greatest hatred. While hatred of other groups has always existed, no hatred has been as universal, as deep, or as permanent as antisemitism."[9]

The Bible tells of two instances where anti-Semitism was so intense that the entire race was threatened: once by a Pharaoh of Egypt (see Exod. 1:8-22) and again by the crafty Haman of Persia (see Esther 3:1-15). Also, on two occasions in more recent history "annihilation campaigns have been waged against the Jews: the Chmielnicki massacres in Eastern Europe in 1648-49, and the Nazi destruction of Jews throughout Europe between 1939 and 1945.[10]

Anti-Semitism has taken the form of actions such as expelling Jews from nearly every country in which they have lived (including England, France, Hungary, Austria, Germany, Lithuania, Spain, Portugal, Bohemia, Moravia and Russia), government and church sanctioned violence against the Jews, beatings, torture, deprivation of property, degradation of every form, restrictions upon education, segregation, execution, murdering of innocent Jewish children (seen in the slaughter of male Jewish children in Bethlehem at the time of Christ's birth—see Matt. 2:16-18—and during the holocaust) and terrorism of unspeakable proportions.

Historical Church Involvement in Anti-Semitism

In the fourth century, there was a change in doctrinal beliefs among Christian leaders which laid the groundwork for later anti-Semitic policies. The teachings of Origen of Alexandria (A.D. 185-254), an early Church father, convinced many that all prophecy was to be interpreted allegorically instead of literally. Hal Lindsey identifies this point of view in his book, *The Road to Holocaust.*

From this seemingly harmless fact of Church history evolved a system of prophetic interpretation that created the atmosphere in which "Christian" anti-Semitism took root and spread.

Using this method of prophetic interpretation, Church theologians began to develop the idea that the Israelites had permanently forfeited all their covenants by rejecting Jesus as the Messiah. This view taught that these covenants now belong to the Church, and that *it* is the only *true Israel* now and forever. The view also taught that the Jews will never again have a future as a Divinely chosen people, and that the Messiah will never establish His Messianic Kingdom on earth that was promised to them.[11]

This particular view of prophetic interpretation led to the Roman Catholic Church's endorsement of the murder of Jews during the crusades of the Middle Ages. The renowned Protestant theologian Martin Luther endorsed anti-Semitism in every form short of annihilation. Following is an excerpt from a tract that Luther wrote in A.D. 1543:

The Bible clearly teaches that, although Gentile believers will share in the fulfillment of God's promises to the Jews, the Jews will not be renounced as God's chosen people and the children of promise.

What then shall we Christians do with this damned, rejected race of Jews?...Let me give you my honest advice: First, to set fire to their synagogues or schools and to bury and cover with dirt whatever will not burn, so that no man will ever again see a stone or cinder of them. This is to be done in honor of our LORD and of Christendom....

Second, I advise that their houses also be razed and destroyed....

Third, I advise that all their prayer books and Talmudic writings, in which such idolatry, lies, cursing, and blasphemy are taught, be taken from them.

Fourth, I advise that their rabbis be forbidden to teach henceforth on pain of loss of life and limb....

Fifth, I advise that safe-conduct on the highways be abolished completely for the Jews....

Sixth, I advise that usury be prohibited to them, and that all cash and treasure of silver and gold be taken from them, and put away for safe keeping....

Seventh, I recommend putting a flail, an ax, a hoe, a spade, a distaff, or a spindle into the hand of young, strong Jews and Jewesses and letting them earn their bread in the sweat of their brow.[12]

It took hundreds of years for deceptive and erroneous theological beliefs to translate into justification for hateful acts of anti-Semitism. The Bible clearly teaches that, although Gentile believers will share in the fulfillment of God's promises to the Jews, the Jews will not be renounced as God's chosen people and the children of promise (see Rom. 11:1-32, especially vv. 17,18,28-31). Erroneous beliefs based on the misinterpretation of Scripture are still with us today, breeding violence and oppression which bears no resemblance to the lives of Christian love we have been called to live.

Some who carry on this tradition of theology which supports anti-Semitism include adherents to British Israelism:

The essence of British Israelism is that people of Northern Europe are the descendants of the Lost Tribes of Israel. They are thus the direct inheritors of the Biblical covenant between God and His chosen people....The largest single British Israel operation in the United States is Herbert Armstrong's Worldwide Church of God.[13]

The Christian Identity Movement, which is growing today in the United States, is an active supporter of anti-Semitic thought. One of the leaders of this movement is Jack Mohr, who heads up an organization called Crusade for Christ and Country.

Mohr commonly shares the platform with local Identity activists and others. Very often his talks are directed at convincing Christians that their own preachers are doing the devil's work by promoting Judeo-Christianity or other "false doctrines." Mohr's favorite themes are the same as those of other Identity speakers: that Jews are children of Satan; that Jesus never was a Jew, but a white Aryan of the Adamic race; that people of color are "pre-Adamic" or beast-like; that northern Europeans are the Lost Tribes of Israel; that America is the promised land; and that Biblical prophecy, including the Armageddon-Tribulation-Rapture story, will be lived out in the U.S., not in the Middle East.[14]

Kingdom Now and Dominion Theology are other forces that promote anti-Semitism. Groups supporting these teachings feel that Christians are responsible to bring in God's Kingdom on earth. Fulfilling this responsi-

23

bility is considered a condition that must be met in order for Jesus to return. They also discount any future messianic kingdom for Israel.[15] Thus they believe the Church takes the place of Israel in God's plan.

These are the types of teachings which form a theological basis (or excuse) for anti-Semitism and manifest themselves in contempt for the Jewish people. They also discourage evangelism of the Jews—an activity which has enjoyed a resurgence since the establishment of Jews for Jesus and a rapidly growing number of Messianic Jewish/Christian congregations. Kingdom Now and Dominion Theology are currently growing in acceptance among some fundamentalist and charismatic churches in the United States.

Why the Jews?

In their essay, "Why the Jews?" Dennis Prager and Joseph Telushkin give a Jewish perspective on what they believe to be the reasons for anti-Semitism. Their four points are summarized as follows:

1. "For thousands of years Judaism has consisted of three components: God, Torah, and Israel; that is, the Jewish (conception of) God, Jewish law and Jewish nationhood."[16] The Jews' allegiance to these three elements has been regarded by non-Jews as a challenge to the validity of their god(s), law and/or national allegiance.

2. The Jews' attempt to change the world and to make moral demands upon others has been a constant source of tension between Jews and non-Jews.

3. The "doctrine of the Jews' divine election has been a major cause of antisemitism."[17]

4. "As a result of the Jews' commitment to Judaism, they have led higher quality lives than their non-Jewish neighbors in almost every society in which they have lived....[This quality of life has] provoked profound envy and hostility."[18]

Throughout history there have also been recurrent lies given as an explanation or excuse to justify anti-Semitism. The most common has been that the whole Jewish race is exclusively responsible for the crucifixion of Jesus (as opposed to the truth that He willingly laid down His life to pay for the sins of the entire world—see Mark 10:45 and 1 John 3:16). The Bible clearly states that Gentiles were also agents of Jesus' crucifixion (see Acts 4:27).

The "blood-libel" accusation that Jews murder non-Jews, especially Christians, in order to obtain blood for the Passover rituals is another lie that was often used to stir up anti-Semitic sentiments. Other charges against Jews have been that they desecrated the host (the bread wafer used in holy communion and believed by many Catholics to be the actual body of Christ) in the desire to inflict again upon Jesus the agonies of the Passion; that they were the cause of various plagues, the Black Death in particular, which ravaged Europe in the fourteenth century; that a worldwide network of Jews were plotting to overthrow the entire free world and set up a world government run by Jews (this is most often substantiated by a fraudulent document titled, *The Protocols of the Learned Elders of Zion*.)[19]

Each of these accusations or variations on these themes have been used throughout history to justify all forms of abuse against the Jews, including execution. These charges are also indicative of beliefs held today by many anti-Semitic groups and individuals.

God promises that whoever blesses Israel will be blessed by God.

Our Response Toward the Jews and Their Oppressors

In general, we should be compassionate toward those who are oppressed (see Ps. 103:6; Isa. 58:9,10; 2 Cor. 1:3,4). Beyond this, going back to the original Abrahamic covenant, God promises that whoever blesses Israel will be blessed by God (see Gen. 12:3). Therefore, in faith, we should make a point of being a blessing to the Jew. It is prudent to consider the fate of all those individuals and nations described in Scripture who lifted up their hands against the Jews. They were severely judged by God or destroyed, as in the case of Pharaoh and Haman of Persia (see Exod. 12:29,30; Esther 7:1-10).

In blessing the Jews, there are many avenues a Christian can take. First, an understanding of the Jewish experience in history and as expressed in the Bible will help develop a sensitivity to the unique challenges Jewish people face. Second, we can support ministries that address and protect the social and spiritual needs of the Jews. Third, we can reach out to Jewish individuals and support and encourage them, sharing the good news God has for them through Christ. Fourth, we can combat influences in our society that promote anti-Semitic beliefs and actions.

We can also learn something from the experiences of the Jewish people. Just as in the past God severely disciplined His people for disobeying His commands, we are warned that we must not become conceited and consider ourselves above them (for further study, see Rom. 9—11, especially 10:12,13 and 11:17-21).

We should be prepared and faithful to present the gospel to all people, including the Jew and the anti-Semite. We are called to be wise, loving, prayerful, hating what is evil but loving those who have been ensnared by the evil one and drawn into a web of hate—all in the name of Christ.

Notes

1. *The Washington Post* (July 14, 1985), p. 11.
2. Nancy Wride, "Odyssey of a Skinhead," *Los Angeles Times* (June 14, 1989).
3. Ibid.
4. "Neo-Nazi Activity Is Arising Among U.S. Youth," *New York Times* (July 6, 1988).
5. William Lawrence Shirer, *The Rise and Fall of the Third Reich* (New York: Simon and Schuster, 1960), p. 105.
6. Ibid., p. 107.
7. Ibid., p. 109.
8. Ibid.
9. Dennis Prager and Joseph Telushkin, "Why the Jews?" *Jewish Almanac and Directory* (New York: Pacific Press, 1986), p. 132.
10. Ibid.
11. Hal Lindsey, *The Road to Holocaust* (New York: Bantam Books, Inc. 1989), p. 8.
12. Ibid., pp. 23, 24.
13. "The Christian Identity Movement: A Theology Rooted in Racism," *The Monitor: Center for Democratic Renewal* (March 1986).
14. Ibid.
15. Louis S. Lapides, The *"Christian Identity" Movement in America.* Prepared for the North American Lausanne Consultation on Jewish Evangelism (April 4-5, 1989), p. 5.
16. Prager and Telushkin, p. 133.
17. Ibid., p. 134.
18. Ibid.
19. Nilus, *The Protocols of the Learned Elders of Zion* (New York: Gordon Press, 1977). Translated and edited by Victor E. Marsden.

TEACHING PLAN

APPROACH (10 minutes)

Materials needed: See each of the activities listed below for specific materials needed and preparation required.

Begin by saying, **Our topic today is anti-Semitism. Anti-Semitism can be defined as hostility toward or discrimination against Jewish people. I want you to see how anti-Semitism has affected real people in this century.** Then brief your students on the holocaust of the Jews that occurred during World War II. Use one of the following activities to present your material.

Activity 1: Show a scene from a movie which describes the persecution of Jews by the Nazis during World War II. Depending on the maturity of your group, choose scenes you feel are appropriate. Some suggested sources you might want to preview include: *The Hiding Place* (a Christian film about the life of Corrie Ten Boom); *Sophie's Choice* (a secular film which is *not* suitable for showing in its entirety or for endorsing—however, there are some powerful scenes near the end of the film where Sophie is forced to give up one of her children to the Nazis); *Genocide* (a film available from the Anti-Defamation League of B'nai B'rith); *The Holocaust* (a made-for-TV mini-series available on videotape—check local video rental outlets).

Activity 2: Invite a survivor (or family member of a survivor) of a Nazi concentration camp to come speak to your group about his or her personal experiences and the effects of anti-Semitism on his or her life. (This will probably take more than ten minutes, so plan accordingly and notify your guest of the time constraints. You may want to ask the survivor to share a short presentation at the beginning and stay to answer questions at the end of the session.) To arrange for such a guest, contact your local chapter of the Anti-Defamation League, a center for holocaust studies, a synagogue or a Jewish/Christian congregation.

Activity 3: Present a dramatic reading of a personal narrative of the effects of anti-Semitism. Some suggested sources include: *Diary of Anne Frank* by Anne Frank; *Voices from the Holocaust,* edited by Sylvia Rothchild; *When Light Pierced the Darkness: Christian Rescue of Jews in Nazi-Occupied Poland* by Nechama Tec. For further resources check the card catalogue of your local library under "Holocaust: Jews."

BIBLE EXPLORATION (30-40 minutes)

Materials needed: Bibles, copies of the "Abrahamic Covenant," "Davidic Covenant," "Palestinian Covenant" and "New Covenant" student worksheets (see Step 1 for more information about how many copies you will need of each of these worksheets), copies of magazine/newspaper articles describing anti-Semitic activities (see Step 3), scratch paper, pencils, chalkboard and chalk or newsprint and felt pen. Optional—one copy of the "Role-play" resource page for every group of four students in your group, snacks, four colors of construction paper, scissors, straight pins or masking tape (see the Alternate Step 4).

Preparation: Optional—cut apart the copies of the "Role-play" resource page along the lines. From construction paper cut badges for your students—cut equal numbers of badges from each color of paper. On each badge draw the following symbols that correspond to the groups of people described on the

"Role-play" resource page—a different symbol on each color of badge (see sketch).

Step 1 (8-10 minutes)

Move the class into groups of two to four (if possible, arrange at least four groups) and distribute pencils and copies of the four student worksheets—one worksheet for each group with an even distribution of the different sheets. Direct each group to read the Scriptures listed and fill in the blanks on the sheet. (Note: The worksheets were designed using the *New International Version* of the Bible. If your students are using a different version, indicate that the wording in their Bibles may vary somewhat.) Then direct the groups to answer the questions at the bottom of the sheet. Allow eight to ten minutes for the groups to work.

Step 2 (7-10 minutes)

Allow time for the groups to share information about each of the four covenants described on the worksheets completed during Step 1. Ask volunteers to share their responses to the questions on their sheets in terms of whether these promises are still in effect, if they still apply to the Jews and how long the covenants will apply to the Jews. As needed to supplement the groups' responses, ask the following questions.

- "Under what conditions will God keep His promises to the Jews?"

- "What do these covenants tell you about God's relationship with the people of Israel?"

- (Read aloud Gen. 12:2,3.) "What does God say will happen to those who treat the Jews with respect and dignity? What will happen to those who oppress the Jews?"

Then explain that much of the justification for anti-Semitic beliefs among Christians depends on the belief that the covenants God made to the Jews have been transferred to another group (such as the Church) and no longer apply to the Jewish people. The reason given for this transfer is that the Jews as a nation were not obedient to God and that they rejected Jesus as the Messiah. Scripture demonstrates that God's covenants with the Jews are based on God's faithfulness, not Israel's performance, and therefore still apply to the nation of Israel. (Refer to Rom. 11:28,29.)

Step 3 (10-12 minutes)

Briefly describe the newspaper/magazine clippings you have gathered of anti-Semitic activities occurring in your area or nation. (Topics might include the activities of white supremecy groups such as the Skinheads and the Ku Klux Klan, or the vandalism of synagogues.)

Direct the students to form groups of four to six (you may want to combine groups formed during Step 1). Provide each group with scratch paper and a copy of one or two of the articles you have gathered.

Direct each group to peruse the articles and then list on a piece of scratch paper reasons why they think the Jews as a group are often oppressed. If possible, be prepared to answer questions about the involvement of such groups in your local area. You may want to share information about anti-Semitic activities and groups that are described in the Teacher's Bible Study. Mention that many of the groups who oppress the Jews do so claiming they are doing "the Christian thing."

Optional—give each group felt pens and a piece of poster board or newsprint and have them illustrate on the poster or paper one reason why they feel the Jews are often oppressed. Allow eight to ten minutes for the groups to work. Then ask volunteers to share their work.

Optional—if you do not have access to articles describing anti-Semitic activities, briefly discuss with your students the reasons listed in the "Why the Jews?" section of the Teacher's Bible Study. Then direct the groups to describe ways people might express in actions and words these reasons for anti-Semitic beliefs.

Step 4 (5-8 minutes)

Say, **As we saw in Genesis 12, God will bless those who are a blessing to the Jews and curse those who oppress them. It is also clearly stated in the New Testament that Christians are to treat others—specifically the oppressed—with love and compassion, and not put themselves above any other group.** (Read aloud, or ask volunteers to read aloud 2 Cor. 1:3,4 and then Rom. 10:12,13.)

Then ask the students to suggest ways they can respond to the oppression that the Jews experience at the hands of other people (including those who call themselves Christians). Ask the students to be specific in describing what they could do. List their ideas on the board or newsprint.

Alternate Step 4 (15-20 minutes)

Use this alternate step instead of Step 4 above if you want to provide your students with a first-hand taste of what

Jewish people have experienced because of anti-Semitism.

Introduce this activity by saying, **We are going to create a setting that will help you experience first-hand some of the feelings and pressures people living in an intensely anti-Semitic environment might have. This will help us evaluate how God would want us to respond to anti-Semitic oppression.**

Move the students into four groups. Label each group with one of the follow designations: "Nazi Police," "Jews," "Ordinary Citizens" and "Christians." Give each student a badge to correspond to his or her group and a straight pin or piece of tape. Also distribute to the members of each group the section of the "Role-play" resource page that corresponds to that group.

Explain the general rules of the role-play as described in the sections of the resource page. (Make it clear that foul language or physical abuse is expressly prohibited. The purpose is to get a *taste* of what the Jews have experienced.) Then allow each group three to five minutes to plan how the group will act out its role within the parameters given on its section of the resource page.

Pass out to all the students the snacks you have brought. Then designate the areas of the room to be used as the Jewish ghetto, the prison and the graveyard. Begin the role-play by having the Nazi police confiscate all food, Bibles and other contraband from the Jews. Have the Nazi police move the Jews into their assigned area. Allow at least five minutes or the amount of time you feel is appropriate for the students to act out their parts and experience the purpose of this activity.

After the allotted time is up, have the students take their seats and share their responses to the activity. To stimulate sharing ask questions such as, **How does it feel to be the object of abuse? Why might those delivering abuse feel they are within their rights to do so? What decisions might an ordinary citizen or Christian be faced with in an anti-Semitic environment?**

Conclude your discussion by asking, **How can Christians respond to the abuse that is often directed at the Jews?** (Read aloud, or ask volunteers to read aloud, 2 Cor. 1:3,4 and then Rom.10:12,13.) Then ask the students to suggest ways they can respond to the oppression that the Jews experience at the hands of other people (including those who call themselves Christians). Ask the students to be specific in describing what they could do. List their ideas on the board or newsprint.

CONCLUSION (3-5 minutes)
Materials needed: Bible.

Reread Genesis 12:3. Then say, **Think of one way you can be a blessing to a Jewish person you know, or a way you can bless the nation of Israel by responding to the oppression of anti-Semitism.** Allow one or two minutes for students to think. You may want to suggest ideas such as supporting a ministry to the Jews, defending Jews when others unfairly criticize or abuse them, telling Jewish people about Jesus the Messiah or praying for and sharing Jesus with peers expressing anti-Semitic beliefs.

Then say, **This week, keep a sensitive ear open to those around you. You may be surprised at how common anti-Semitic feelings are. Be prepared to respond in the way you have chosen.**

THE ENVIRONMENT

GLEN WOLFE

KEY VERSES

"God blessed them and said to them, 'Be fruitful and increase in number; fill the earth and subdue it. Rule over the fish of the sea and the birds of the air and over every living creature that moves on the ground.'...The Lord God took the man and put him in the Garden of Eden to work it and take care of it." Genesis 1:28; 2:15

BIBLICAL BASIS

Genesis 1:26,28,31; 2:15; 3:17-19; Leviticus 25:3-5, 8-12; Deuteronomy 23:12,13; 28:1-8,15,38-42; 2 Chronicles 7:13,14; Psalm 8:3-8; 19:1-4; 136:1-9; Luke 12:6,7; John 6:12

FOCUS OF THE SESSION

God has given humankind the responsibility of taking care of the earth.

AIMS OF THIS SESSION

You and your students will have accomplished the purpose of this Bible study session if you can:

- DESCRIBE the role God has given people in relationship to His creation;
- DISCUSS ways people can respond responsibly to environmental abuses;
- PLAN one way to make a difference in caring for God's creation and PRAY asking God's help in healing the abuses to creation.

TEACHER'S BIBLE STUDY

God and Creation

God created a wonderful place for us to live. He could have created a humdrum world with just the bare necessities, but He didn't. He created a world full of beautiful colors, fragrances, sounds and a great variety of plants and animals (see Gen. 1:1-26). God created everything for His glory (see Isa. 43:7), but He also created the earth for the enjoyment of humankind as well as His other creatures (see Gen. 2:8,9). God, being very pleased with His creation, proclaimed that it was good (see 1:31).

The Bible shows that God cares deeply about the intricate details and the everyday activities of His creation. He values each and every creature. Christ says in Luke 12:6,7, "Are not five sparrows sold for two pennies? Yet not one of them is forgotten by God. Indeed, the very hairs of your head are all numbered. Don't be afraid; you are worth more than many sparrows."

In His wisdom, God has provided humankind with some guidelines for conservation and waste disposal as a means to protect His creation (see Lev. 25:1-12; Deut. 23:12,13). Jesus personally condemned unnecessary waste (see John 6:12). Because of His personal concern for His creation and the role creation plays in displaying His glory, God must be displeased when His beloved creation is abused or mistreated (you may want to read the curse Simeon and Levi received in response to their cruelty to people and animals—see Gen. 49:5-7).

Man and His Relationship to Creation

Men and women were created in God's image. "As lovely, beautiful, colorful, and full of variety as the plant or animal kingdom may be, none of that has been created in God's image, only human life."[1] God gave people dominion over all the animals and everything in the earth: "Let us make man in our image, in our likeness, and let them rule over the fish of the sea and the birds of the air, over the livestock, over all the earth, and over all the creatures that move along the ground" (Gen. 1:26; see also 2:19,20).

Humankind was given the commission to populate the earth and take control of it (see 1:28; the Hebrew word used here is *kabash* which means to "master," "subdue" or "take control of") as well as to take care of it (see 2:15). Both responsibilities go hand-in-hand and balancing between the two can be difficult. Yet this balance is necessary, for the protection of the environment and for meeting the needs of people.

Some champions of the environment in our day refuse to accept the biblical concept that God created the earth for persons. For some, the earth, not God, is eternal. Persons are only partners with other life forms, not "rulers" over creation. Some advocates of "deep ecology" view the earth itself as a living organism (often called "Gaia")—a pantheistic view that denies any difference between Creator and creation.[2]

Although God is perfect and created a perfect world, creation and humankind's dominion over the earth were dramatically impacted by Adam and Eve's rebellion against God in the Garden of Eden. In Genesis 3:17-19, God declares the consequences of their actions: "Cursed is the ground because of you; through painful toil you will eat of it all the days of your life. It will produce thorns and thistles for you, and you will eat the plants of the field. By the sweat of your brow you will eat your food until you return to the ground, since from it you were taken; for dust you are and to dust you will return."

It can be surmised that Adam and Eve's rebellion against God is the root of many of our current environmental problems. The reason behind this is the tension their disobedience created between people and the land of which they are stewards. Disharmony with God created disharmony in creation. There would be no need for weed killers (against thorns and thistles overtaking the ground—see v. 18) if it hadn't been for the fall of humankind. And the effort required for harvesting needed food would have been greatly reduced.

God did, however, promise His people prosperity in their agricultural pursuits if they honored and obeyed Him and respected and cherished His creation (see Deut. 28:1-14; 2 Chron. 7:13,14). God also warned that if His people didn't honor and obey Him and respect and cherish His creation, their efforts with the land would be unsuccessful (see Deut. 28:15-24).

Our prayers of repentance and our obedience to God can result in healing in our environment. We are responsible to obey God and be good stewards of His creation. But we can also look forward to the day when God will release the earth from its bondage instituted at the Fall (see Rom. 8:18-25; Rev. 21:1).

Although God is perfect and created a perfect world, creation and humankind's dominion over the earth were dramatically impacted by Adam and Eve's rebellion against God in the Garden of Eden.

The Pollution of Our World

The fall of humankind in the Garden of Eden had a dramatic effect on our ability to have dominion over the earth and to be able to take control of it. People have been able to use their God-given gifts through science to develop substances such as insecticides which have returned to us some sense of dominion over the earth. If it weren't for insecticides, insects would probably dominate and we might have a difficult time growing enough food for our people.

However, some of the first successful insecticides and other man-made molecules have created problems in our struggle for dominion. These substances are not biodegradable as natural substances are. When a leaf dies it breaks down into its basic building blocks and is reused. Not so with some synthetic molecules such as DDT, PCB, chlorofluorocarbons (refrigerants) and many plastics. These indestructible molecules persist in the environment, often continuing year after year poisoning God's creation.

DDT is an insecticide which nearly wiped out the pelicans and other wildlife.[3] DDT was banned in 1972 in the United States, but it still persists in the environment although its concentrations in human fatty tissue are declining. In 1970 the concentration of DDT in this "adipose" tissue of people in the United States was eight parts per million. In 1983 the concentration was two parts per million.[4] DDT has been replaced by new, improved biodegradable insecticides which do their job and then are gone, but there are still serious questions concerning their safety.[5]

Carbamates, chemicals frequently used in insecticides and weed killers, threaten wildlife because they sometimes convert to cancer-causing compounds in the stomachs of mammals. Agriculture today uses nearly twice the volume of pesticides and herbicides spread in 1964. These poisons travel on the wind or percolate into the groundwater, affecting our environment beyond their intended, local purposes. The estimated global sales of pesticides in 1975 equaled $5 billion. The estimated global sales of pesticides projected for 1990 are $50 billion. Over half of these sales are for home use.[6]

Other substances which are poisoning our environment are metals such as mercury, copper and lead. By examining human remains in 500-year-old graves, researchers found that Greenland Eskimos today have in their bodies three to seven times the mercury, copper and lead their ancestors carried.[7]

Lead shot buried in wetlands still threatens many varieties of birds.[8] These levels of lead poisons can be reduced as sportsmen switch to steel shot.

In another arena of nature, New England crabs have been found to have burn marks on their shells from a disease believed caused by heavy metals in ocean water.[9]

Furthermore, half of the carbon dioxide we dump into the atmosphere is absorbed by single-celled plant life in the oceans. These phytoplankton are easily poisoned by carbon dioxide and certain metals.

Other villains are chlorofluorocarbons. Chlorofluorocarbons, used as refrigerants and in aerosol cans, are thought to be destroying the ozone layer of the atmosphere. The ozone layer protects us from overdoses of ultraviolet light which cause sunburn, skin cancer and further destruction of plant life.[10]

Poisons created from the burning of fossil fuels are causing major changes in our environment. Fossil fuels (gasoline, oil, coal) contain sulfur. When they are burned the sulfur becomes a gas (sulfur dioxide). Nitrogen oxides are also produced from the combustion of gasoline. All of these gases can be carried by the wind for hundreds of miles. When it rains, these

poisonous gases dissolve in the rain water and become acid rain.[11] Acid rain is responsible for the destruction of structures, forests, fish and many varieties of wildlife. One can just look at a balsam forest in North Carolina or a forest almost anywhere and see the destruction caused by acid rain.

The main pollutants produced by the burning of fossil fuels—sulfur dioxide, oxides of nitrogen, hydrocarbons and ozone—are harmful to our lungs as well as to the environment in general. The only way we can prevent some of this destruction is to cut back on our use of fossil fuels. All in all, despite tougher antipollution legislation, the plight of our air, water and wildlife has worsened in the last 20 years.[12]

A World Out of Balance

God created a world in balance. There have always been wastes produced by metabolic processes, but God in His magnificent ecological engineering has created ways to recycle these wastes. Plants take in the carbon dioxide produced by the respiration of animals and convert it back to sugar and water.

Humankind, however, has caused the natural balance to be disrupted. The average person contributes over 20 times more carbon dioxide by driving his or her automobile than he or she personally breathes out into the air. People dump 6 billion tons of carbon dioxide into the atmosphere every year.[13] At the same time we are killing off plant life with pollution and with the removal of vegetation for the development of cities and freeways.

The result is that normal processes are no longer capable of removing the wastes we are producing. The accumulation of these wastes is causing dramatic changes in our environment.

One evidence of this change is that the earth is gradually warming. By A.D. 2030 our summers could be 10 degrees warmer and the Rocky Mountains might be without snow in the winter. This warming of the earth, called the greenhouse effect, may result in a reduction in the amount of rain the earth will receive. This could change some of our fertile areas into deserts.

Due to the melting of the ice caps, the ocean levels are slowly rising. This may mean that some cities such as Miami, Florida and New Orleans, Louisiana could be under water in the next few decades. This could

Authorities say that we cannot prevent the world from warming up and cannot minimize the repercussions that will be involved.

cause the destruction of the homes of 20 million people in the United States alone.[14]

The world's energy consumption is rising as the world's population increases. In 1970, the world's human population was 3.72 billion. The world population estimated for 1990 is 5.32 billion.[15] The total world carbon emissions from the burning of fossil fuels in millions of metric tons in 1970 was 3,934. In 1986 it was 5,225.[16]

Whenever we light a fire, drive a car or turn on a light, we contribute carbon dioxide to the atmosphere. Electricity is generated, for the most part, by the burning of coal and other fossil fuels. Over half the electricity consumed in the United States is powered by coal. The percentage is much larger in other parts of the world.[17]

The burning of coal is the worst culprit in the destruction of our environment. The burning of coal contributes twice the amount of carbon to the atmosphere as the burning of natural gas. Yet many countries such as China are planning to increase their use of coal in the next few years.[18]

Authorities say that we cannot prevent the world from warming up and cannot minimize the repercussions that will be involved. "Even if we replaced every tree that has been cut down in the last century and stopped using fossil fuels, the temperature would continue to rise until all the trees were full grown."[19]

What we can hope for is that we can slow the rate of change enough so we have time to adapt to the catastrophic changes caused by the warmer weather. For example, much of the world will starve unless we can buy time to develop varieties of wheat, corn and other crops that can survive longer, drier growing seasons. Whole cities may also have to be moved inland. We need to buy time to be able to make these changes, and each of us can help.[20]

What We Can Do

The saving of God's creation must be a priority in each of our lives or the consequences will be catastrophic. We need to conserve our plant life, reforest, drive less and use a lot less energy. Recyling helps in a number of ways. In Portland, Oregon alone, 2,000 fewer trees a day would be cut down if subscribers to the *Oregonian* newspaper would recycle their newspapers.[21] Sixty to 95 percent less energy is needed to recyle paper, metal and glass as compared to the energy needed to manufacture them from virgin materials.[22] For every glass jar that's recyled, the energy conserved would illuminate a light bulb for four hours. At present, however, only 10 percent of the metal and glass being produced in the United States is being recycled.[23]

We can become active in groups which are implementing workable solutions for saving the environment. An example of such a group is River Watch, a school-based program that originated in Montpelier, Vermont. "River Watch currently has student volunteers monitoring water pollution levels across the United States."[24]

Six years ago a fledgling ecology club at Casa Grande High School in Petaluma, California began cleaning up the trout stream at Adobe Creek, which had been polluted and neglected. They even built their own fish hatchery, and today Adobe Creek is healthy and alive with trout.[25] This and many other examples show that teenagers can make a big difference when it comes to saving God's creation.

Our prayers are as essential as any other conservation technique. With such delicate balances involved, it is easy to see the importance prayer can have on our future environment. God, who created the world, can also heal it—either through our obedient efforts, or by a miracle. As 2 Chronicles 7:14 implies, God can intervene, using the healing of nature as a reward for our prayers and obedience to Him: "If my people, who are called by my name, will humble themselves and pray and seek my face and turn from their wicked ways, then I will hear from heaven and will forgive their sin and will heal their land."

Human sin certainly includes neglecting God's creation with all our dumping of wastes and poisons—forgetting our responsibilities as stewards of the earth. But if we repent, try to correct our abuses and pray, we can trust God to reward our efforts.

Our prayers are as essential as any other conservation technique.

Notes
1. Charles R. Swindoll, "Why I Stand for Life," *Focus on the Family* (August 1990), p. 19.
2. Loren Wilkinson, "New Age, New Consciousness, and the New Creation," *Tending the Garden* (Grand Rapids, MI: Wm. B. Eerdmans Publishing Co., 1987), p. 22.
3. Karen Arms, *Environmental Science* (Troy, MO: Saunders College Publishing, 1990), p. 22.
4. Chris Willis, "Vital Statistics," *National Wildlife* (February/March 1990), p. 3.
5. Peter Steinhart, "Innocent Victims of a Toxic World," *National Wildlife* (February/March 1990), p. 22.
6. Willis, p. 33.
7. Steinhart, p. 22.
8. Ibid., pp. 25, 26.
9. Ibid., pp. 20, 21.

10. Arms, p. 65.
11. Steinhart, p. 24.
12. Sharon Begley, "Toxic Pollutants Pose a Far Greater Threat than Anyone Imagined," *National Wildlife* (February/March 1990), p. 47.
13. Arms, p. 72.
14. Ibid., p. 66.
15. Willis, p. 33.
16. Ibid.
17. Arms, p. 189.
18. Ibid., p. 72.
19. Ibid.
20. Ibid.
21. Lisa Graham McMinn, "Taking Care of God's Earth," *Virtue* (May/June 1990), p. 29.
22. Ibid.
23. Ibid.
24. Michael Johns, "River Watch," *Campus Life* (April 1990), p. 39.
25. Katrine Ames, "Kids with Causes," *Newsweek: Special Issue* (Summer/Fall 1990), p. 65.

TEACHING PLAN

APPROACH (2-3 minutes)

Materials needed: Bible.

Introduce this session by saying, **God created a wonderful place for us to live. He created a world full of beautiful colors, fragrances, sounds and a great variety of plants and animals. Consider a beautiful, scenic place. This special spot may be a forest, a mountain area, waterfall, river or a favorite campsite. Think about what such a scenic place tells you about God.** Allow time for three or four volunteers to share their thoughts. Then read aloud Psalm 19:1-4. **What do these verses say is the role of creation?** (To give praise and glory to God.)

Move to the Bible Exploration by saying, **Today we are going to take a look at our role in taking care of what God has created.**

BIBLE EXPLORATION (35-45 minutes)

Materials needed: Bibles, a copy for each student of the "Creation: God's Gift, Our Responsibility" and "What We Can Do" student worksheets, copies of newspaper/magazine clippings that describe current environmental problems, pencils, chalkboard and chalk or newsprint and felt pen. Optional—a copy for every two students of the "Let's Debate" resource page. Materials described in Step 2.

Preparation: Optional—cut the copies of the "Let's Debate" resource page in half (see the Alternate Step 3).

Step 1 (12-15 minutes)

Move the students into groups of four to six. Distribute pencils and copies of the "Creation: God's Gift, Our Responsibility" student worksheet. Direct half of the groups to complete the "God and Creation" section of the sheet and direct the remaining groups to complete the "People and Creation" section. Allow eight to ten minutes for the groups to work.

Reassemble the large group and discuss the groups' responses to the questions on the worksheet. You may want to list their responses on the chalkboard or newsprint. After reviewing the worksheet ask, **Why do you think it is difficult for people to balance their role as rulers over creation with their responsibility as preservers of creation?**

Step 2 (8-10 minutes)

Distribute copies of one or two magazine/newspaper clippings to each group. Give the groups two or three minutes to peruse the clippings and summarize the environmental concern described in their articles. Allow time for the groups to share the information they have gathered from the clippings. As needed, describe some of the key environmental concerns discussed in "The Pollution of Our World" and "A World Out of Balance" sections of the Teacher's Bible Study.

Move to Step 3 or the Alternate Step 3 by saying, **It is difficult to know how we can take control and rule over the earth and yet not abuse God's creation. Let's look at ways we can respond to this situation.**

Step 3 (15-20 minutes)

Direct the students to return to their groups of four to six. Distribute copies of the "What We Can Do" worksheet. Instruct each group to choose one area listed on the sheet that describes a way the group is interested in helping preserve God's creation. Share the story of the River Watch group described in the "What We Can Do" section of the Teacher's Bible Study.

Then say, **Plan an advertising campaign to promote your plans to preserve or restore the environment. You may plan ways to use different forms of media, organizations or individual action to accomplish your goals. Be prepared to present your plan to the group.** Allow 10 to 15 minutes for the groups to work. Optional—provide the groups with materials to help them begin their campaigns (tape recorders and blank cassette tapes, poster board and felt pens, the names and addresses of organizations or government agencies they might want to contact).

Allow time for the groups to present their campaigns. Then discuss the following questions: **What limits do you think need to be placed on our right to subdue, or control, the earth? To what extent do you think we should be active in preserving God's creation?**

Alternate Step 3 (10-15 minutes)

Use this alternate step instead of Step 3 above if you feel your students will benefit from a verbal debate of points of view on an environmental issue.

Direct the students to move into two groups. (Note: If you have a large class, choose six volunteers to represent the "Pro" position and six volunteers to represent the "Con" position. The remainder of the students will be the audience of the debate.)

Place the two groups so they are facing each other. Distribute the "Pro" portion of the "Let's Debate" resource page to each member of the "Pro" group, and the "Con" portion of the page to the each member of the "Con" group (see the Preparation). Give each group one minute to review the information on the page.

Then ask the "Pro" group to respond to the question, "Should we try to save endangered species?" Give the group two minutes to express its views based on the information on the resource page. Then ask the "Con" group to respond to the question, giving them the same two-minute time limitation. If you have students in the "audience" who would like to comment "pro" or "con," allow time for them to do so.

When the time is up, discuss the tension that exists when dealing with environmental issues. Ask questions such as, **What are some specific things a person could do to address the issue of endangered species? What are some other environmental concerns that teenagers can address? How can a teenager be involved in this area? What limits do you think need to be placed on our right to control the earth? What limits should be placed on preserving God's creation?**

CONCLUSION (3-5 minutes)

Materials needed: Bible, newsprint and felt pen or chalkboard and chalk.

Work together as a group to create on the chalkboard or newsprint an environmental prayer list. Say, **Prayer and obedience to God as good stewards of the earth are two ways we can participate in bringing healing to our environment.** Refer to 2 Chronicles 7:13,14.

Then lead your students in a time of prayer by giving the following directions: (1) **From the list we have made, choose one area in which you want to make a difference in caring for God's creation;** (2) **Prayerfully ask God to show you one way you can show care for His creation in the area you have chosen;** (3) **Ask God to help you follow through on your desire to obey Him and be a good steward of the world He has entrusted into our care.** Allow time after each direction for students to silently reflect and respond.

Close in audible prayer, praising God for displaying His glory through creation. Ask for His help to appreciate the earth He has given us and to care for it wisely.

 FOR A 13-WEEK TEACHING PLAN

If you are teaching on a 13-week quarter system, you may want to choose from the following suggestions to extend this session over two weeks.

During your next meeting after teaching this session involve your students in a group outing that will reinforce the need to appreciate and care for God's creation. This could include cleaning up around the church building, gathering materials for recycling, visiting a scenic spot and having a time of praise and appreciation for what God has made.

See page 10 of this book for further information.

MEDIA VIOLENCE

TOM NASH

KEY VERSE

"'In your anger do not sin': Do not let the sun go down while you are still angry." Ephesians 4:26

BIBLICAL BASIS

Psalm 72:12-14; Proverbs 14:29; 15:18; 19:11; Isaiah 59:1-8; Matthew 5:43,44; Romans 12:18; 13:1-5; Galatians 5:20,22,23; Ephesians 4:31,32; James 1:19-20; 4:1-3

FOCUS OF THE SESSION

Media violence both reflects and adds to the problem of violence in society. As Christians, we need to learn to appropriately express anger and control our intake of violent media.

AIMS OF THIS SESSION

You and your students will have accomplished the purpose of this Bible study session if you can:
- EXAMINE what the Bible says about violence and expressing anger;
- DISCUSS ways media violence can affect a person's ability to control anger;
- PLAN ways to modify personal media habits and methods of handling anger.

TEACHER'S BIBLE STUDY

Violence is a common theme in the popular mass media—especially in television, films and music. By "violence" we mean aggressive acts which physically hurt or kill people or threaten to do so.

Even though it has been known for some time that violence in the media causes viewers to become more aggressive, the number of violent episodes on the air remains high. Researchers reported that 80.9 percent of all television shows contained some violence, and that the average number of violent acts per program was 4.98.[1]

Because the violent parts of television shows are usually fast moving and intense, they are particularly likely to hold the attention of viewers, increasing their impact.

The impact of violence portrayed on television is especially significant because the average household has the set on about seven hours a day, according to the A.C. Nielson company.[2] However, films, music videos and rock music must also be considered as influential because many contain high levels of violence.

A great deal of research has been done over the years about the effects of media violence. There is now little doubt that watching violence makes people more prone to act aggressively.

In a United States Senate hearing in 1972, Surgeon

General Steinfield summarized the data on media violence: "There is a causative relationship between televised violence and subsequent antisocial behavior."[3] Research since then has continued to demonstrate that exposure to media violence produces violence in viewers.

Brian Wilcox, testifying in May of 1989 on behalf of the American Psychological Association before the House of Representatives, identified four specific effects of media violence. These are:

1. Copycat violence which occurs when people learn and mimic behavior seen on the screen.

2. Removal of inhibitions concerning aggression and increased likelihood of committing violent acts.

3. Desensitization in the area of value development. Because of exposure to media violence, people become less sensitive to the effects of violence when they view it in the real world. Real-world violence becomes more accepted as normal.

4. Exaggerated fear of violence. People believe the world is far more violent than it really is.[4]

Media is not the only factor that influences violent behavior. Family, school, church and social settings are actually far more influential in promoting or inhibiting violence. Still, the media is a consistent, powerful influence toward violent behavior.

There is now little doubt that watching violence makes people more prone to act aggressively.

Why Does Violence Sell?

Since the negative effects of violence in media are generally accepted by researchers, why does the high level of violence continue?

Broadcasters historically defend their programming choices on the basis of giving the audience what it wants. Fundamentally broadcasting is business, designed to deliver large audiences to advertisers in order to make a profit. Motion picture and record companies also try to produce what they believe will sell. Violence sells. If people stopped watching and listening to violence, media producers would stop producing it.

Many governments are reluctant to interfere in media programming because of "freedom of speech" considerations.

What Does the Bible Say About Violence?

The story of humankind, as told in the Bible, is a bloody story. The Bible could be considered a violent book because it tells the truth about the nature of humanity. Many terrible atrocities are recorded. But this does not mean that God approves of such behavior. Quite the contrary, God condemns those who shed innocent blood. Isaiah describes God's feelings: "Your iniquities have separated you from your God; your sins have hidden his face from you, so that he will not hear....Their deeds are evil deeds, and acts of violence are in their hands. Their feet rush into sin; they are swift to shed innocent blood" (Isa. 59:2,6,7; see also Ps. 72:12-14).

Manasseh brought punishment on the nation of Judah because he "had filled Jerusalem with innocent blood, and the Lord was not willing to forgive" (2 Kings 24:4). God allowed raiders from surrounding areas to attack Judah, destroy the country and remove them from His presence (see v. 3).

Even David, a man after God's own heart (see Acts 13:22), was judged for his violent deeds. God said David could not build His Temple because David had "shed much blood on the earth in my sight" (1 Chron. 22:8).

While the Bible permits governments to use the sword to bring about justice (see Rom. 13:1-5), God clearly desires that His followers, as much as possible, live peaceful lives (see 12:18).

Where Does Violence Come From?

James 4:1-3 reveals the ultimate source of violence: "What causes fights and quarrels among you? Don't they come from your desires that battle within you? You want something but don't get it. You kill and covet, but you cannot have what you want. You quarrel and fight. You do not have, because you do not ask God. When you ask, you do not receive, because you ask with wrong motives, that you may spend what you get on your pleasures."

When we desire something that we are not allowed, we experience an unpleasant feeling called "frustration." If frustration over selfish wants becomes quite intense we call it "anger." This kind of anger is a powerful feeling directed at the person or agency that we believe is keeping us from getting what we want.

Anger is a very normal emotion experienced by all people. Sometimes people claim they never feel angry, but they are deceiving themselves. Even God feels anger (see Deut. 11:16,17; Judg. 2:12-14; Neh. 9:17). But while God's anger is always justified, sometimes our anger is not. The emotion is not sinful, but how we let the emotion influence our thoughts and behavior can be.

Controlling Anger

Even though anger is natural and normal, it can also be dangerous. If we allow anger to take over, we can do many foolish, harmful and dangerous things. The Bible gives us at least four ways to deal with anger appropriately.

First, we need to realize that uncontrolled anger is sinful. The Bible never tells us it is wrong to experience anger, but it does tell us we must control what we do as a result (see Heb. 12:14,15). Ephesians 4:26 summarizes this point well: "In your anger do not sin." Galatians 5:20 lists "fits of rage" as an act of the sinful nature, while Galatians 5:23 lists "self-control" as a fruit of the Spirit. Christians have the power of God's Spirit to help them control their anger.

Second, we need to take time to evaluate our emotions and motives before expressing anger. Proverbs tells us repeatedly that we should be patient rather than hot-tempered (see 14:29; 15:18; 16:32; 19:11). James 1:19,20 expresses this same idea: "Everyone should be quick to listen, slow to speak and slow to become angry, for man's anger does not bring about the righteous life that God desires." The old idea of counting to ten before you express anger is a step in the right direction in dealing with anger in a godly manner.

Third, forgiveness is an essential element in dealing with anger. Ephesians 4:31,32 contrasts rage with forgiveness: "Get rid of all bitterness, rage and anger, brawling and slander, along with every form of malice. Be kind and compassionate to one another, forgiving each other, just as in Christ God forgave you."

Others will offend us and justly and unjustly deny us what we want and deserve. We must learn to forgive them just as God has forgiven us.

In the parable of the unmerciful servant (see Matt. 18:21-35) Jesus tells of a servant who was forgiven a large, virtually unpayable debt. Soon after receiving forgiveness for this debt, this servant refused to forgive a small debt owed him by a fellow servant. When the master got wind of what had transpired, stiff punishment was administered to the unforgiving servant. If we realize how much God has forgiven in us, we will understand the injustice of an act of anger or violence against another.

The principle of forgiveness is also emphasized in the Lord's prayer: "Forgive us our debts, as we also have forgiven our debtors" (Matt. 6:12). God expects and requires us to forgive those who wrong us. If we truly forgive those who have wronged us, we no longer have just cause for expressing angery emotions toward them. Thinking about how much God has forgiven (and is forgiving) us compels us to forgive others! (See vv. 14,15.)

A fourth biblical principle for controlling anger is sacrificial love. This involves giving up our own rights for the benefit of someone else out of obedience and love for God. The primary example of sacrificial love is Jesus. He set aside His rights and privileges in heaven to come to earth and die an unjust death of torture for our sake.

If we try to see people the way God does, we will understand how valuable each person is—even if they are miserable, disgusting sinners who treat us badly. To

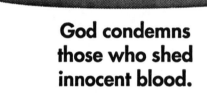

God condemns those who shed innocent blood.

the extent we are controlled by God's Spirit, we will be able to let God's love reach out through us. If our priorities are eternal we will be more able to deal with losing the things that seem precious in this world without letting our anger turn into violence.

While all Christians struggle to control inappropriate expressions of anger, younger Christians will probably have more difficulty. Young people often have intense emotions but less experience in controlling them than older, more mature Christians. A high degree of idealism is also typical of young people. The realities of life in a sin-cursed world often create intense frustration and anger that can seem overwhelming.

Young people, because of their limited experience with life, tend to be "now" oriented. The concept of waiting for justice—days, months or even until the final judgment—is harder for them than for adult Christians. You will need to help your students identify practical ways to manage angry feelings and respond to frustrating situations with the fruit of the Spirit rather than acts of their sinful natures. Their exposure to violence in media is an obvious starting place.

What's Wrong with Media Violence?

Watching or listening to violence in the media can work against learning to deal with anger God's way. The reasons for this include:

1. Violence is often presented in the media as the best or only solution available. In life violence is rarely the

best or only solution. However, if a person is only aware of a violent solution, he will tend to use it.

2. In the media, the by-products of violence are portrayed unrealistically. People die instantly and cleanly. The hero never shoots the wrong person or gets fatally shot himself. And the hero suffers no remorse. The violent solution is shown as unrealistically easy and attractive.

3. Media often promotes unrealistic expectations about how long it takes to solve problems. On television, major problems are resolved in 30 or 60 minutes; in films resolution takes about 90 minutes. People with an excessive diet of media will become extremely frustrated when they find that major life problems may take weeks, months or years to resolve. Some are never solved.

4. Popular forms of media rarely emphasize biblical values or means for solving problems. We hardly ever hear a hero pray for divine guidance. Forgiveness and self-sacrifice are rare. Usually protagonists use human means to achieve human ends. Christians who expose themselves too much to this kind of thinking may forget they are participating in spiritual warfare and have spiritual resources available to them!

Forming a Plan for Media Use

Mass media can be a powerful master or powerful servant. The choice is ours. Either we control the media or it controls us! We can control the media by prayerfully and thoughtfully choosing what we watch, read and listen to. Here are some suggestions that will help your students battle the negative affects and influences of media violence:

1. Plan in advance your use of different mediums. Break the habit of just plopping down in front of the TV and watching whatever is on at the moment! Use a television guide, and spend some time each week deciding which programs are worth seeing and which are not. Choose movies carefully, paying attention not only to the MPPA rating system (G to R), but also to what Christian reviewers have to say (several Christian youth magazines write reviews on current media expressions—films, music, TV).

2. Limit media exposure. The media should complement, not dominate, your life. If you find the media using up a large percentage of your free time, break the habit.

Make friends, play sports, take up a hobby or volunteer to help in a soup kitchen. Don't let media control your life.

3. Read more, watch TV and movies less. Reading gives you more control. There are many more books available than TV shows. You can pick them up, put them down and turn pages when you want to. Choose books wisely, though, since they can be as violent and sexy as other media!

4. Take advantage of Christian media. There are Christian radio and television stations in many communities; Christian videos, records, books and films are available as well.

5. Discuss the content of the media you are using. Don't just uncritically absorb non-Christian values. You might consider watching TV or going to a movie with some Christian friends. Have pizza afterwards and talk about what was right and wrong about the value assumptions of the movie.

> If our priorities are eternal we will be more able to deal with losing the things that seem precious in this world without letting our anger turn into violence.

Changing the Media

As the language on television has become increasingly foul, a defense media people have often used is that nobody seems to care! If we as Christians care about profanity, obscenity, excessive violence or sexuality in the media, we need to let the media producers know.

Most media executives are not horrible, hard people. Some are even Christians. If they receive thoughtful, respectful letters and phone calls from individuals and groups they will usually respond and often will make changes. They need to know we care. Encourage your students to communicate with the local media regularly when they see or hear something they feel is inappropriate.

Additional Preparation

If you (like many adults) seldom, if ever, attend youth-oriented movies or listen to teen-oriented radio or MTV, you may wish to expose yourself a bit to these mediums prior to presenting this lesson. Then you can share firsthand what you have experienced. This should help your credibility with your students and should give you a much better idea of what you are talking about!

Notes

1. I. Pearl, L. Bouthilet and J. Lazar, eds., *Television and Behavior: Ten Years of*

Scientific Progress and Implications for the Eighties, Vol. 2 (Washington, D.C.: United States Government Printing Office, 1982), pp. 158-174.
2. *National Audience Demographics Report* (A.C. Neilson Company, 1976).
3. United States Senate Hearing (1972), p. 28.
4. United States House of Representatives hearing (May 1989).

TEACHING PLAN

APPROACH (5 to 8 minutes)

Materials needed: Scratch paper, pencils, chalkboard and chalk or newsprint and felt pen.

Introduce this session by saying, **A good number of films and television stories depict someone who gets into a bad situation and then gets out by using some kind of violence—like killing or injuring another person. What are some TV shows or movies where this has happened?** Allow time for three or four students to share.

Move students into groups of two to three. Distribute scratch paper and pencils to the groups. Say, **In your groups, discuss how the kinds of TV shows and movies we have talked about are different from real life. List on your scratch paper as many differences as you can.** Circulate among the groups to see how they are doing. After about three minutes, have the groups report their findings. Summarize their ideas, listing them on the chalkboard or newsprint.

Move to the Bible Exploration by saying, **Today we are going to look at what the Bible says about violence and how popular forms of media violence can affect the way we deal with real life.**

ALTERNATE APPROACH (5-8 minutes)

Materials needed: Costume ideas as suggested in the Preparation.

Preparation: Before class, ask an outgoing student (or adult counselor) to prepare to role-play the part of a person from the imaginary island of Mambo-Pambo. Provide him or her with a silly island costume to wear (bright print shirt, straw hat with plastic fruit, etc.). Tell your volunteer that he or she will tell the class what he or she knows about your country based on what he or she has seen by satellite TV on Mambo-Pambo. The volunteer should present a very distorted picture such as: in this country all problems are solved by killing people and that nobody minds when people are killed; everybody drives real fast and reckless and wrecks up a lot of cars; most of the police are crooked; all problems can be solved in half an hour; and women are beautiful, but weak and dumb.

Introduce your island guest by saying something like

this: **Class, we have a special guest today. This is (name). He/she has lived all of his/her life on the tiny island of Mambo-Pambo. This is his/her first visit to our country. Let's welcome him/her.** (Lead in applause and cheers.)

The guest says he or she actually knows quite a lot about the country because our television is beamed to Mambo-Pambo by satellite. Then have the guest share his or her description of life in your country. Thank your guest for sharing. Then ask, **Is this what life is like here?** Lead a short discussion on the difference between real life and life as depicted in the media.

Move to the Bible Exploration by saying, **Today we are going to look at what the Bible says about violence and how popular forms of media violence can affect the way we deal with real life.**

BIBLE EXPLORATION (25-35 minutes)

Materials needed: Bibles, a copy for each student of the "How to Control Anger" student worksheet, pencils, chalkboard and chalk or newsprint and felt pen.

Step 1 (5-8 minutes)

Lead a discussion about violence by asking, **How would you define violence?** (People killing, hurting or threatening themselves or other people.) **Why do you think people use violence as a way to solve their problems? What do you think is the source of violent actions?**

Then present a brief lecture about violence in the media and what the Bible says about acts of violence. Include in your presentation the following points and any additional information from the Teacher's Bible Study.

- In a United States Senate hearing in 1972, Surgeon General Steinfield summarized the data on media violence: "There is a causative relationship between televised violence and subsequent antisocial behavior." Research since then has continued to demonstrate that exposure to media violence produces violence in viewers.

- Brian Wilcox, testifying in May of 1989 on behalf of the American Psychological Association before the House of Representatives identified four specific effects of media violence: copycat violence; removal of inhibitions concerning aggression; desensitization to violence when viewed in the real world; and an exaggerated fear of violence.

- Broadcasters historically defend their programming choices on the basis of giving the audience what it wants.

- The Bible could be considered a violent book because it

tells the truth about the nature of humanity. But this does not mean that God approves of such behavior. Quite the contrary, God condemns those who shed innocent blood. (Ask volunteers to read the following verses: Ps. 72:12-14; Isa. 59:1-8.) Ask, **How do these verses express God's attitude toward wrongful violence?**

• While the Bible permits governments to use the sword to bring about justice, God clearly desires that His followers, as much as possible, live peaceful lives (Ask volunteers to read Rom. 13:1-5, and then 12:18.)

Step 2 (5-10 minutes)

Ask a student to locate and read from the Bible James 4:1-3. Ask, **What do these verses say cause violence?** Then work together to list on the board or newsprint the steps involved in a person expressing violence (desire, frustration from not receiving what you want, feelings of anger, acting out anger through quarreling and violent acts). As needed, share additional information from the "Where Does Violence Come From?" section of the Teacher's Bible Study.

Summarize your list by saying, **The basic cause of violence seems to be an inappropriate reaction to feelings of frustration and anger.** Point out that the Bible does not condemn any human emotion, even anger. But if anger gets out of control it may lead a person to do sinful things. Refer to Ephesians 4:26. Then move to Step 3 by saying, **Let's look at what we can do to keep feelings of anger under control.**

Step 3 (8-12 minutes)

Move the students into groups of four to six. Distribute pencils and copies of the "How to Control Anger" student worksheets. Direct the groups to work together to complete the top portion of the page. After five minutes gather students' attention and briefly review and discuss their answers to the questions on the worksheet. You may want to include in your discussion information from the "Controlling Anger" section of the Teacher's Bible Study.

Step 4 (4-5 minutes)

Say, **The information you have researched on controlling anger can be summarized by four simple principles.** Refer students to the statements in the "Four Things We Can Do to Control Anger" section of their "How to Control Anger" worksheets. Ask volunteers to suggest words that they feel will complete each of the statements (pray for self-*control*; be *slow* to anger; *forgive* the person who wronged you; *love* your enemies). As needed, comment briefly on each of the four points.

Point out that controlling anger is not easy. You might want to share a brief anecdote of a time you blew it badly. Ask students to suggest ways you could have handled the situation using the principles presented on the "How to Control Anger" worksheet. As necessary, point out to your students what was sinful and harmful about your actions and what was not.

Step 5 (7-10 minutes)

Lead a discussion on the subject of how media violence can affect a person's ability to control anger. As needed, supplement your discussion with material from the "What's Wrong with Media Violence?" section of the Teacher's Bible Study. Ask, **How does the media tend to portray the expression of feelings of anger? How does the media unrealistically present violent expressions of anger? What expectations for solving problems could a person on a heavy diet of media violence have? In what ways are Christian values presented in the media as a means of dealing with anger?**

Call your students' attention to the fact that a constant diet of media violence is going to make it very difficult, if not impossible, for a person to learn to control anger. The reason for this is because in the media anger is usually not controlled.

CONCLUSION (3-5 minutes)

Materials needed: A copy for each student of the "My Personal Media Use Plan" student worksheet, pencils, chalkboard and chalk or newsprint and felt pen. Optional— copies for each student of the names and addresses of television stations, radio stations and major book, music and movie distributors who do business in your area.

Preparation: On the chalkboard or newsprint write the following questions. Keep them from the students' view until you are ready to refer to them.
1. What will make it difficult for me to follow my media use plan?
2. What will help me follow it?
3. Why is it important that I follow it?

Distribute pencils and copies of the "My Personal Media Use Plan" worksheet. Say, **Let's take a look at our own media habits and plan ways we can honor God through our use of the media.** Direct students to individually complete their worksheets. As needed to help students complete the page, share information from the "Forming a Plan for Media Use" section of the Teacher's Bible Study. As students work, complete a worksheet of your own.

When students have completed their worksheets,

39

direct their attention to the questions you have written on the newsprint or chalkboard. Share with the students how you would personally answer each question. Then direct them to prayerfully consider these questions and ask God to direct them in their use of different mediums.

Close in audible prayer, asking the Lord to help each student follow his or her media plan.

Optional—distribute the names and addresses of television stations, radio stations and major book, music and movie distributors that do business in your area. Suggest that your students write letters to these media representatives, pointing out offensive business practices (employees at video rental stores recommending R rated or violent videos to minors, violent programming on public airwaves—especially during hours when minors are most likely listening/viewing, etc.) and program content. Emphasize that the letters must be specific (date and specific information about the offending material or business practice and why it is offensive), accurate and respectful.

 **FOR A 13-WEEK TEACHING PLAN**

If you are teaching on a 13-week quarter system, you may want to choose from the following suggestions to extend this session over two weeks.

At the end of this session give your students one of the following assignments: (1) For one or two evenings, keep count of the number of TV shows you watch. When watching, keep count of the number of times an act of violence is used to resolve a situation and the number of times a peaceful solution is used to resolve a situation. (2) Count the number of songs on the recordings (records, cassettes, CDs) you personally own. Read through the lyrics of each song on each recording and keep tract of the number of songs that support the use of violence against self or another person. Calculate the percentage of the songs you have that support violence compared to the total number of songs in your collection.

During your next meeting after giving these assignments, discuss the students' findings and their feelings about what they have discovered. Have a time of sharing about real-life situations where your students must make decisions about expressing anger appropriately. Resource that can help stimulate discussion in this area include *Outrageous Object Lessons* and *The Youth Worker's Book of Case Studies* (see p. 127 for more information about these and other resources).

See page 10 of this book for further information.

HOMELESSNESS

GAIL NELSEN

KEY VERSE

"I know that the Lord secures justice for the poor and upholds the cause of the needy." Psalm 140:12

BIBLICAL BASIS

Psalm 139:13-16; 140:12; Proverbs 17:5; Matthew 25:34-40; Luke 4:18,19; James 2:3-9

FOCUS OF THE SESSION

By sharing God's concern for the needs of the homeless, we are expressing our gratitude for God's love for us.

AIMS OF THIS SESSION

You and your students will have accomplished the purpose of this Bible study session if you can:

- DESCRIBE how God feels about the plight of the homeless;
- LIST ways Christians can address the causes of homelessness and the needs of homeless people;
- CHOOSE an action you can take to respond to the needs of the homeless.

TEACHER'S BIBLE STUDY

Who Are the Homeless and How Many?

In the past, a homeless person was typically depicted as an alcoholic street transient, deranged bag lady or dirty beggar. These people were often dismissed with no thought at all.

Cases like these still exist and need care, but we must understand that homelessness, especially in the United States, has changed. It is estimated that as many as four million or more Americans may currently be homeless.[1] An increasing number of these people are referred to as the "new homeless." Jonathan Kozol in his book *Rachel and Her Children: Homeless Families in America* states:

Since 1980 homelessness has changed its character. What was once a theater of the grotesque...has grown into the common misery of millions.

"This is a new population," said a homeless advocate in Massachusetts....In Massachusetts, three-fourths of all homeless people are now children and

41

their parents. In certain parts of Massachusetts...90 to 95 percent of those who have no homes are families with children.[2]

We need to begin seeing that the homeless can't be lumped together in one group. People who find themselves homeless fall into many categories and families must now be included. The poor, the hungry and the "new homeless" must all be recognized. The longer they are on the streets or fighting to stay in their non-affordable homes, the more their human spirits become disfigured and their hope diminishes.

Why Are People Homeless?

Because we tend to group the homeless together and become overwhelmed by their need, we often get caught up in the task of providing beds and overlook the cause of their plight. Meeting the immediate needs of the homeless is necessary, but it often comes at the expense of long-term solutions. The causes of homelessness must not be overlooked because they are, in essence, the solution to the problem. In part, the reason for society's short-sightedness may come from its inability to provide a place for those people that cannot compete economically.[3]

Mary Ellen Hombs and Mitch Snyder feel that:

The poorest of the poor—the homeless—are literally on the streets, without resources and absent any choices save those that promise survival....We live in a disposable society, a throwaway culture. The homeless are our human refuse, remnants of a culture that assigns a pathologically high value to independence and productivity. America is a land where you *are* what you consume and produce. The homeless are simply surplus souls in a system firmly rooted in competition and self-interest, in which only the "strongest" (i.e., those who fit most snugly within the confines of a purely arbitrary norm) will survive.[4]

In addition to society's general difficulty with valuing the homeless, there are four primary areas that are generally believed to contribute heavily to the plight of the homeless. (1) steady increases in the rates of unemployment and underemployment; (2) a crisis in the availability of affordable housing; (3) poorly planned deinstitutionalization of the mentally unstable; (4) reductions in government poverty and disability programs.

Of these four areas, Jonathan Kozol feels that the shortage of affordable housing is the dominant cause of homelessness today. He says: "Unreflective answers might retreat to explanations with which readers are familiar: 'family breakdown,' 'drugs,' 'culture of poverty,' 'teen pregnancies,' 'the underclass,' etc. While these are precipitating factors for some of the people, they are not the cause of homelessness. *The cause of homelessness is lack of housing.*"[5]

The history of the United States government's sponsorship of affordable housing is one illustration of the increasing severity of this problem. Over the years, federal funding for public housing has been greatly reduced. This withdrawal of funds is partially responsible for the lack of new affordable housing and the disintegration or conversion of existing buildings in low income areas. Because many cities are left with virtually no affordable housing, often low income people are left without alternatives.[6]

> Meeting the immediate needs of the homeless is necessary, but it often comes at the expense of long-term solutions.

God's Perspective

To respond to the cause of homelessness from a Christian perspective, we must first examine our common human condition and God's concern and care for every person. If we correctly understand the "sameness" of all people, it might make a difference in how we as Christians relate to the homeless. This sameness provides Christians with a common foundation by which to cross barriers that might otherwise divide them from the homeless.

The foundation all people share is one of being known and loved by our Creator and the need to have an intimate relationship with this One who loves us so perfectly. Rich or poor, we all share this common heritage and should esteem each other as equals. Luke 12:7 says that "the very hairs of your head are all numbered." And Psalm 139:13,14 says, "For you created my inmost being; you knit me together in my mother's womb. I praise you because I am fearfully and wonderfully made." Just as we can praise God for His wonderful work in creating us, we can praise Him for His work in creating the homeless, the poor, the dirty and the mentally unstable who we may judge to be lesser persons.

God understands our tendency to spurn those we consider undesirable, especially the poor and destitute, and He bluntly states that this tendency is not to be indulged: "He who mocks the poor shows contempt for their Maker" (Prov. 17:5). Our attitude toward God is reflected in our attitude toward the poor.

As we delve more into Scripture we see that we are commanded to do more than adjust our thinking toward the poor and homeless. We are called to take action, to reach out to those we tend to discriminate against. James 2:3,4 says that when we show favoritism to the rich at the expense of the poor we have "become judges with evil thoughts." The solution to avoiding the sin of showing favoritism is to "love your neighbor as yourself" (v. 8). Loving implies reaching out to our neighbor beyond our self-interest or fear—without regard to who or what that neighbor might be.

Scripture clearly declares that God is looking out for the poor; He has a special concern for them and their plight. Psalm 140:12 says, "I know that the Lord secures justice for the poor and upholds the cause of the needy." Jesus declared that God's purpose in sending Him to humankind was to "preach good news to the poor. He has sent me to proclaim freedom for the prisoners and recovery of sight for the blind, to release the oppressed, to proclaim the year of the Lord's favor" (Luke 4:18,19).

Considering God's care for us all and His special concern for the poor, we need to obey His command to love those in need. God's command to love is not general and abstract. He backs His command up with specific ideas individuals can use to minister to the needy. In addressing the issue of fasting with the purpose of making their hearts right before God, Isaiah 58:6,7 describes actions by which the people should express their repentance:

"Is not this the kind of fasting I have chosen: to loose the chains of injustice and untie the cords of the yoke, to set the oppressed free and break every yoke? Is it not to share your food with the hungry and to provide the poor wanderer with shelter—when you see the naked, to clothe him, and not to turn away from your own flesh and blood?"

Matthew 25:37-40 also describes the relationship between God's love for us and our response to His love expressed in helping the less fortunate:

"Then the righteous will answer him, 'Lord, when did we see you hungry and feed you, or thirsty and give you something to drink? When did we see you a stranger and invite you in, or needing clothes and clothe you? When did we see you sick or in prison and go to visit you?'

"The King will reply, 'I tell you the truth, whatever you did for one of the least of these brothers of mine, you did for me.'"

> Just as we can praise God for His wonderful work in creating us, we can praise Him for His work in creating the homeless, the poor, the dirty and the mentally unstable whom we may judge to be lesser persons.

What Can We Do?

There are a variety of ways Christians can address the problem of homelessness in both long-term and short-term ways. Some channels may be by political means, social action and spiritual outreach. Democratic societies allow individuals to participate in establishing government policy, therefore those with such opportunities can use this obvious means of addressing the causes of homelessness.

We can get to know a homeless family and assist them into housing; we can advocate better job training and job placement for the poor; we can demand a higher minimum wage; we can lobby for affordable housing in our cities; we can work to establish homes for the mentally ill; we can establish and advocate poverty and disability programs; we can assist with child care while a family is getting established.

While we labor in soup kitchens, work to renovate buildings into low income housing and provide shelter beds, we can become advocates for long-term solutions as well. The poor need the support of our public voices. As the Body of Christ we can combine merciful emergency services while working for the elimination of homelessness. Showing immediate mercy is love but so is working for the elimination of the root causes.

Conclusion

Micah 6:8 sums up God's perception of how His people are to live in relation to others and Himself: "He has showed you, O man, what is good. And what does the Lord require of you? To act justly and to love mercy and to walk humbly with your God."

We are to be just and work for justice as we humbly walk with God. Justice is defined in *Webster's Ninth New Collegiate Dictionary* as "the quality of being just, impartial, or fair...the principle or ideal of just dealing or right action...righteousness...correctness."

Getting to know, accept and share with the homeless, and beginning to work on behalf of the poor, will cause us to see opportunities to correct injustice in our land. To act justly is to use our authority, power, money, clout and any other resources to uphold what is right in relation to the needs of the homeless. We must address the root causes as we get to know the homeless poor, begin to be their friends and seek to alleviate their suffering. To advocate on behalf of those who cannot is the work of justice.

Can the Church of Jesus Christ respond to the needs of the homeless? The Church can and must. But the road to transforming our thinking is very long. One of the reasons transformation is so difficult is because of barriers. One barrier Christians often have to overcome is the isolation of the poor from the non-poor. The poor and the non-poor do not hang around together. Alice Frazer Evans, in her book *Pedagogies for the Non-Poor,* describes this isolation. She feels that lack of understanding for the poor on the part of the non-poor is a result of lack of exposure. The non-poor cannot empathize with the suffering of poor people with whom they do not have contact. [7]

If Christians are to take Jesus seriously, we will have to go out of our way to get to know those less fortunate than ourselves. Getting to know the poor is a transforming process. It is the first step toward making the necessary changes in our thinking. Personal experience with those suffering injustice holds us accountable and demands response.

> **As the Body of Christ we can combine merciful emergency services while working for the elimination of homelessness.**

Notes

1. Jonathan Kozol, *Rachel and Her Children: Homeless Families in America* (New York: Crown Publishers, Inc., 1988), p. 10.
2. Ibid., pp. 4,5.
3. Kim Hopper and Jill Hamberg, *Making of America's Homeless: From Skid Row to New Poor 1945-1984* (New York: Community Service Society of New York, 1984).
4. Mary Ellen Hombs and Mitch Snyder, *Homelessness in America: A Forced March to Nowhere* (Washington, D.C.: Community for Creative Non-Violence, 1982, 1983, 1986), p. 4.
5. Kozol, p. 11.
6. Christopher Coons and Keith Summa, "Decent Homes for all Americans," *Seeds Magazine* (December/January, 1987, 1988), p. 14.
7. Alice Frazer Evans, *Pedagogies for the Non-Poor.* (Maryknoll, NY: Orbis Books, 1987), p. 260.

TEACHING PLAN

APPROACH (10 minutes)

Materials needed: Posters or pictures depicting the plight of the hungry and homeless, chalkboard and chalk or newsprint and felt pen. (Note: Organizations that address homelessness and the plight of the poor often have literature and pictures available to the public. You may want to contact your local office of the United Way or another organization established in your community.)

Optional—a recording of the song "Homeless" by Paul Simon and a means by which to play the recording.

Display or distribute the posters and/or pictures you have gathered. Encourage students to share their experience with or exposure to the topic of homelessness by asking the following questions: **Have you ever met a homeless person or family? How would you describe your experience? Do you know anyone who is poor? How many homeless people are there in our country? Let's make a list of reasons why you think some people are homeless.**

List students' ideas on the chalkboard or newsprint. As needed, share information from the "Why Are People Homeless?" section of the Teacher's Bible Study. Also share any information you may have gathered about the homeless situation in your community.

Optional—play a recording of the song "Homeless" by Paul Simon.

Make a transition to the Exploration by asking volunteers to share how they think they might feel if they had nowhere to go to sleep tonight.

BIBLE EXPLORATION (25-35 minutes)

Materials needed: Bibles, a copy for each group of four to six students of the "God's Perspective" resource page, scratch paper, pencils, chalkboard and chalk or newsprint and felt pen. Optional—poster board and felt pens, a copy for each student of the "Music Madness" student worksheet, a recording of Phil Collins' song "Just Another Day in Paradise" (or another recording that describes how God feels about the struggle of the poor and/or homeless), a means by which to play the recording (see the Optional Step 3 for details).

Step 1 (10-12 minutes)

Say, **Before we can respond effectively to the problem of homelessness, we must first look at how God feels about the homeless and how He wants us to respond to their situation.** Move the students into groups of four to six and distribute pencils and copies of the "God's Perspective" resource page. Assign each group one assignment from the page to complete, then allow eight to ten minutes for each group to work. Optional—you may want to provide groups completing Assignments 2 and 3 with poster board and felt pens.

Step 2 (10-15 minutes)

Gather the attention of the students and ask each group to share its work. (Note: If you have a large number of students or limited time, ask groups to volunteer to share. Include responses from groups that worked on each of the three assignments.) As each group shares, discuss the following questions.

Assignment 1: What makes each person unique and worthwhile to God? How can God's opinion of the homeless influence your feelings toward them? What advice can you give a person who struggles with accepting the homeless and poor as valuable and equal to all other people created by God?

Assignment 2: Why do you think God is specifically concerned about the needs of the poor and homeless?

Assignment 3: What reason for not helping the poor and homeless do you think Christians use most often? What do you think really keeps Christians from caring for the poor and homeless? How does a Christian's perspective of who the homeless are and what they are like affect their motivation to help?

If you do not choose to complete the Optional Step 3, move to Step 4 by saying, **When we see the poor and homeless as God sees them, we are motivated to take action to help alleviate their plight. Let's look at ways Christians can help the homeless.**

Optional Step 3 (10-20 minutes)

Offer one or both of the following activities if you want to integrate drama and/or music in this session.

Act It Out: Direct students to work in groups of five or more to create modern dramatizations of James 2:1-9. Allow five to eight minutes for the groups to work, then ask them to share their dramatizations. After the groups have shared ask, **How does God feel about favoritism and prejudice? What command does God want us to follow? How can loving others as God has loved us help us understand and accept the poor and homeless?**

Music Madness: Distribute copies of the "Music Madness" student worksheet to students. Play a recording of Phil Collins' song, "Just Another Day in Paradise" (or another recording that describes how God feels about the struggle of the poor and/or homeless). Direct students to answer the questions on the worksheet as they listen to the song. After the song has played, ask volunteers to share their responses to the questions.

Move to Step 4 by saying, **When we see the poor and homeless as God sees them, we are motivated to take action to help alleviate their plight. Let's look at ways Christians can help the homeless.**

Step 4 (5-8 minutes)

Refer to the causes of homelessness that you listed during the Approach. Ask, **What are some things our group could do to address the problem of homelessness?** List students' suggestions next to the causes. For more information about working toward solutions to homelessness, see the "What Can We Do?" section of the Teacher's Bible Study. Then ask, **Which of these actions will have an immediate impact on a person's homeless situation? Which of these actions will have more of a long-term affect in improving the plight of the homeless?** Point out that the homeless are in need of both immediate and long-term aid. Balancing our efforts between both kinds of aid will help Christians more effectively advocate for solutions to homelessness.

Note: Helping the homeless in ways that effectively meet their needs can be challenging. Some efforts, though well intentioned, may not be the best avenues to follow. It is helpful to begin ministering to the homeless by working through established organizations and people who are well-acquainted with successful methods of helping the homeless.

CONCLUSION (10 minutes)

From the information shared during Step 4 of the Bible Exploration, ask students to individually choose one action they want to take to respond to the needs of the homeless. Ideas might include: reading liturature to educate themselves about the plight of the homeless, volunteering to help in a soup kitchen, writing letters to political leaders in their community and national capitol about their concern for the homeless, etc.

Ask volunteers to pray, thanking God for His provision of homes and specific items in their homes that they enjoy (suggestions: stove to cook on, food, bathroom, bed, blankets, sink and water to wash with, washer for clothes, phone, electricity, place to dress, clothes, refrigerator). Close by asking God to help each person find ways to minister to the needs of the homeless.

Optional—as a class plan a group effort to address the problem of homelessness. Ideas might include: make buttons advocating help for the homeless to pass out at church; adopt a homeless family and provide groceries for them; have a movie night at church to educate your congregation on the subject (you may want to preview the secular film *Ironweed* for this pur-

pose—see your local video rental store); sponsor a work day at a local shelter.

For a 13-Week Teaching Plan

If you are teaching on a 13-week quarter system, you may want to choose from the following suggestions to extend this session over two weeks.

During your next meeting after teaching this session, arrange for your group to visit a homeless shelter, serve in a soup kitchen or have a representative from an organization that ministers to the needs of the homeless speak to your students.

See the article, "How to Use This Course" on page 8 of this book for further information.

PUT-DOWNS

TOM FINLEY

KEY VERSE

"Therefore encourage one another and build each other up, just as in fact you are doing." 1 Thessalonians 5:11

BIBLICAL BASIS

Genesis 1:26,27; Proverbs 16:24; Galatians 6:7-10; Ephesians 4:29; 1 Thessalonians 5:11; James 3:7-10

FOCUS OF THE SESSION

God wants us to use language that will build others up.

AIMS OF THIS SESSION

You and your students will have accomplished the purpose of this Bible study session if you can:
- EXAMINE the Bible's instructions regarding speech;
- DISCUSS ways to build others up;
- CHOOSE a specific person and PLAN a way to build that person up.

TEACHER'S BIBLE STUDY

Your students are masters of the put-down. What is a put-down? It's an insult, a cruel remark or even a well-intentioned joke at someone's expense. Perhaps you remember a time in high school when you had your hair cut or styled. The silly comments you heard may have ranged from the unoriginal ("You got your ears lowered") to the faintly humorous ("I've seen more hair on a piece of bacon"). Hopefully, these put-downs were offered in a spirit of tongue-in-cheek friendliness. But not all put-downs are meant to be friendly. And even those intended to be friendly can be taken as offensive. Such comments can be stunningly cruel ("You're so fat you have to use a belt for a watch-band").

High school students can, intentionally and unintentionally, be cruel and insensitive. This session focuses on reversing this situation. You and your students will examine Bible verses that tell exactly how God expects us to manage our mouths. By applying God's wisdom, your students can not only put the brakes on tasteless put-downs, they can actively build up and encourage others.

Why Put-downs?

Why do we put people down? There are several reasons. First and foremost, we are self-centered sinners. When a person sins, he or she misses the mark or is not on target, centered on God and what He wants. One aspect of sin is being self-centered rather than God-centered. And being egotistically self-centered creates a desire to build our own selves up. We often do this by putting others down. This is absurd reasoning because the best way to have yourself built up is by building up others. But this reasoning is a common expression of a person's sin nature.

Some people put others down because they themselves feel down. A person with a bad self-image seeks to compensate for his or her feelings of inadequacy. This compensation can take many forms, including attempts to bring others down to his or her perceived level. Ironically, a person with a poor self-image desperately needs others to build him or her up!

Another reason kids put others down is because of the insecurity they are feeling as they struggle for independence from their parents. In every family with children, there comes a time when the parents' apron strings must be cut. This severing does not happen overnight and there is often a bit of struggle along the way. This struggle is another reason for put-downs. Kids flare up at their seemingly overly strict parents, while grownups put their children down for their disobedience and lack of support. Unfortunately, being sinful by nature, we pollute God's plan of growing up and leaving home with expressions of anger and resentment.

On the other side of the coin, there are put-downs that are given good-naturedly and are meant to be taken that way. Good friends often joke at each other's expense. Unhappily, it is not always possible to know when we overstep the bounds of innocent fun. During counseling, married couples will often complain that something meant as a joke was taken as hurtful by a partner.

In each of these instances we can readily imagine how replacing a put-down with a "build-up" would create a healthier relationship and meet each person's need for esteem. We've already said that the best way to have yourself built up is to build up others. People like nice people! A person with a poor self-image can attract compliments by giving them away. Family members can continue to enjoy good relationships as children grow toward independence if parents and children will encourage each other by word and deed. Good natured put-downs, if there really are such things, should always be augmented by sincere compliments and affection.

What the Bible Says

Proverbs 16:24 says, "Pleasant words are a honeycomb, sweet to the soul and healing to the bones." This verse reveals the positive nature of build-ups. The children of Israel in Bible times would dream of sweet, wild honeycomb. Happy was the weary traveler who stumbled upon this special treat, for it was both tasty and refreshing.

Pleasant words, according to this verse, are tasty and refreshing. That is, they make us feel good and are tangibly good for us. Compliments draw people together; insults drive them apart. Compliments build up a person's self-esteem; insults tear down. Compliments encourage people to achieve more; insults discourage them from trying. You can test this for yourself by remembering your reaction the last time a student thanked you for a great Bible study!

Ephesian 4:29 is similar to Proverbs 16:24, but it adds a new thought: "Do not let any unwholesome talk come out of your mouths, but only what is helpful for building others up according to their needs, that it may benefit those who listen." The new thought is that speaking pleasant words is an act of the will. According to Paul, the author of Ephesians, it is possible for our words to be unwholesome rather than pleasant. He commands us to forbid the unwholesome words from leaving our lips.

Our own day-to-day experiences teach us that there is nothing automatic about speaking in compliments. Consider those times you accidentally said something you didn't really mean. Were your words a put-down or a build-up? Ninety-nine times out of a hundred, our unthinking comments are negative. How many times have you accidentally complimented someone?!

Therefore, we all must concentrate on guiding our speech towards good. Bad habits can be broken. Put-downs can be replaced with build-ups. It simply takes practice, as Ephesians 4:29 reminds us.

Another thought Ephesians 4:29 shares is that our build-ups are not to be empty words. They are to be based on the needs of the person we are addressing;

> ## The best way to have yourself built up is to build up others.

they are intended to "benefit those who listen." Compliments that are not appropriate are not believed and therefore discarded. They also create suspicion that future compliments also are not sincere.

First Thessalonians 5:11 says, "Therefore encourage one another and build each other up, just as in fact you are doing." Here we see Paul putting his own advice into action. After commanding the Ephesians to encourage and build up one another, he compliments them on the fine job they are already doing! Isn't it good to see a preacher practice what he preaches? You, too, must build up and encourage your students as you teach them to do the same. As you know, we teach more by our actions than by our words. Your students will follow your lead.

Put-downs betray a lack of respect. Even if we can find nothing to compliment in people, we can treat them with the respect due anyone who is made in the image of God (see Gen. 1:26,27). And if we're Christians, a slanderous tongue certainly is no credit to our own claim to be created *anew* (see Col. 3:8-10). According to James 3:7-10, the tongue that honors God in one breath and puts down a person in the next is totally inappropriate.

How to Build Others Up

There are principles involved in applying God's command to encourage and build up others. Here are some ideas to consider.

1. Know what people like and need to hear. In a survey conducted by *Brio* magazine, girls were asked what they wished guys knew about them and guys were asked what they wished girls knew about them. Among other things, the girls said they wished boys knew they were extremely sensitive about their looks and weight. They also enjoyed being treated like a lady, not punched playfully in the arm. The boys said they loved to be complimented and it killed them when they were made fun of for something they said or did.[1] If you are aware of another's soft spots and needs, you will know how to compliment and build that person up.

2. Be sincere. Remember Eddy Haskell on the old "Leave It to Beaver" show? One of his famous lines went something like, "My, Mrs. Cleaver, what a lovely dress you are wearing." Everyone, including Mrs. Cleaver, knew that Eddy was a cad. His words rang hollow. A sincere compliment builds up while hypocritical flattery "will get you nowhere" as the old saying goes.

3. Show appreciation. A person who does a job without receiving thanks or recognition will tend to become discouraged. Simply saying thank you can encourage a person and turn a tedious chore into something meaningful.

4. Invite others to join you. One of the best ways to build a person up is to extend an invitation to join you in an activity. This gesture tells a person that they are important to you. This action should be repeatedly emphasized in church youth groups. Ask your students to raise their hands if they eventually came to Christ because someone thoughtfully invited them to come to a group activity. There will be many hands.

5. Apologize the proper way. Have you ever heard an apology something like this? "I'm sorry I yelled at you, but I was just so mad after what you did...." The person then describes the horribly offensive thing you did. That's not a real apology! It's a recrimination disguised as an apology. It certainly doesn't help heal the wounds, does it? A true apology does not seek to excuse one's behavior by shifting the blame. A true apology says, "I'm sorry. Can we be friends?" That sort of apology builds up, brings together and heals broken relationships.

6. Consider the person from God's perspective. All people are created in the image of God (see Gen. 1:26,27). Approaching a person with respect because he or she is a creation of God will allow you to build the person up—even if he or she has not done anything for which you can administer a compliment. Your reasons for building a person up are not dependent on that person's actions, but his or her worth in God's eyes.

The Boomerang Effect

One of the nice things about following the scriptural injunction to build up and encourage others is that, in so doing, we will be built up. By replacing put-downs with build-ups, we can enjoy popularity and build close friendships. Communicate these truths to your students. By doing this, you'll be building them up as God commanded.

> **Even if we can find nothing to compliment in people, we can treat them with the respect due anyone who is made in the image of God.**

Note
1. Susie Shellenberger, "What Girls Wish Guys Knew About Them/What Guys Wish Girls Knew About Them," *Brio* (March 1990), p. 24.

TEACHING PLAN

APPROACH (6-8 minutes)

Materials needed: Scratch paper and pencil for each student. Optional—inexpensive reward (gift certificate, munchies).

Begin this session by saying something like this: **Let's play a simple game I call "Compliment Wars." The object is to be the first to write a valid compliment for each person in the room.**

Distribute paper and pencils. If your students want to know what sort of compliments you mean, tell them to think of nice things they could honestly say to their classmates. The point of the game is to get students thinking about the topic of building others up. (If you have a small number of students, have each player list two or more compliments per student.)

After three or four minutes, discuss the compliments—but do not use the names of students in connection with the compliments (to prevent anyone from feeling left out if his or her name isn't mentioned). Help students distinguish between valid and invalid compliments. (Valid compliments are honest and build the person up. Invalid compliments exaggerate and do not build a person up.) Have students review their lists and cross out any invalid compliments. Optional—recognize the student who thought up the greatest number of valid compliments and award him or her a reward.

If students joke that it was hard to think of nice things to say about the people in class, use that as a springboard to introduce the lesson. Move to the Exploration by saying, **I had you play this game as a sort of test. I wanted to see if you needed to polish up your complimenting skills. Today's topic is building others up, something the Bible talks about in detail.**

ALTERNATE APPROACH (5-6 minutes)

Materials needed: Scratch paper and pencils.

Move students into groups of two or three and distribute scratch paper and pencils. Ask each group to list three put-downs they've heard or used. For example, almost everyone has heard large feet referred to as "banana boats." Each group should define what its three put-downs mean (or you can have groups switch

> A sincere compliment builds up while hypocritical flattery "will get you nowhere."

papers for this part of the activity).

After three or four minutes, discuss the various put-downs and how they make the people receiving them feel about themselves.

Move to the Bible Exploration by saying, **These put-downs can sometimes be meant as harmless jokes. But they can also be used as arrows to wound others. The Bible has much to say about the opposite of put-downs, things we could call "build-ups." Let's take a look at what the Bible can teach us.**

BIBLE EXPLORATION (35-50 minutes)

Materials needed: Bibles, a copy for each student of the "Put-downs Vs. Build-ups" student worksheet, pencils, chalkboard and chalk or newsprint and felt pen, one or two packets of seeds (lima beans or another large-sized seed will work best).

Step 1 (8-10 minutes)

Assemble the students into groups of two to four. Distribute pencils and copies of the student worksheet. Have the members of each group work together on the "Bible Build-ups" section of the worksheet.

After four or five minutes gather the students' attention. Ask volunteers from the groups to tell what the verses they read say about how we should talk to others. List their responses on the chalkboard or newsprint. Be sure that each of the items listed below is included in the responses you write on the board or newsprint.

- Pleasant words are healthy.
- No unwholesome talk is to be allowed.
- Helpful words are desired.
- We are to build others up with our speech.
- We are to encourage each other.
- It is wrong to praise God in one breath and put someone down in another.

Ask, **What do these verses tell you about how God feels about put-downs?** Read aloud Genesis 1:26,27. **What is one reason these verses give for building another person up?** (The person has been created by God and in His image. He or she should be treated with respect.) **How do these verses help you build up someone who is difficult to compliment? Let's think of specific things we can say that will build others up the way God has commanded us.**

50

Step 2 (12-15 minutes)

Direct students to return to their original groups. Assign to each group one or two of the case studies from the "Sound Familiar?" section of their worksheets. (Optional—if you prefer, complete this assignment together as a class discussion.) Encourage the groups to think of practical, detailed solutions to their assigned case studies.

After about ten minutes, have each group share its ideas for one or two of the case studies it discussed. Talk about how the people might feel when complimented or encouraged, and how their feelings might affect their behavior and their attitudes toward themselves and others. Optional—those groups that feel comfortable doing so may role-play their ideas for one or more of the case studies on the worksheet.

Ask students if they have faced any situations similar to the case studies described on the worksheet. Encourage volunteers to share what happened and how they felt during the situation. Be prepared to share an experience of your own.

Move to Step 3 by saying, **We've come to understand that compliments can build people up in such a way that not only are their feelings uplifted, but their very behavior and self-image can be changed for the better! But there is another side to building up others: the boomerang effect. Let's look at how it works.**

Step 3 (5-10 minutes)

Illustrate the meaning of Galatians 6:7-10 by presenting the following object lesson. Show students the packets of seeds you have brought. Open a packet and, if appropriate, toss a few seeds out where the students are sitting. Say, **If I plant lima beans, chances are I will reap a harvest full of lima beans—probably more beans than I planted! The same goes for words. If I seed my conversation with hurtful words, what will I reap?** Allow for a response. **If I sow encouraging, helpful words into my conversations with others, what will I receive in return?** Allow for a response. **Often we put others down in an attempt to build ourselves up. These attempts always backfire because of the boomerang effect: What we send out comes back—and can knock us over on the way, destroying what little self-esteem we may have. The Bible says that we will reap what we sow.** Read aloud Galatians 6:7-10. **If we need to feel better about ourselves, one of the best things we can do is help others feel better about themselves. God promises that our efforts will somehow be rewarded by others building us up—it becomes contagious!**

If students feel comfortable doing so, ask one or two

volunteers to share about a time they built someone else up. Ask, **How did encouraging that person make you feel about yourself? How did the person you helped respond?** Mention that you may not get positive results every time you build someone up. But if you make a habit of it, people will soon think of you as an encouraging, helpful person. Being a "builder-upper" will create opportunities for you to make friends that will support and encourage you. And God will use these experiences to help you feel good about yourself. Then move to Step 4 or the Alternate Step 4.

Step 4 (10-15 minutes)

Move the students into groups of four to six—each group should be made up of all girls or all guys. Direct the groups of girls to list on the backs of their worksheets valid compliments or build-ups they like to hear from guys; the groups of guys should list valid compliments or build-ups they like to hear from girls.

After five to eight minutes, have volunteers share their groups' lists. Discuss how these build-ups fulfill what the Bible passages studied say and how they might help the person being built up. Ask, **How are guys different from girls in terms of the ways each likes to be built up?** Allow several moments for the guys and girls to debate this question.

Move to the Conclusion by saying, **We've seen how following the Bible's instructions to build a person up can help that person feel good about him- or herself. Now let's plan a specific way we can build someone up this week.**

Alternate Step 4 (10-15 minutes)

You may want to complete this alternate step instead of Step 4 if you used the Alternate Approach at the beginning of the session. Have students work in their groups to rewrite as build-ups the put-downs they listed during the Alternate Approach. For example, a put-down such as, "I see you got your ears lowered" could be turned into a compliment such as, "I like your hair. Who styled it for you? Maybe I could have mine done like that, too."

After five to eight minutes, have students share their build-ups. Discuss how these build-ups help fulfill the commands in the Bible passages studied and how they might help the person being built up.

Move to the Conclusion by saying, **We've seen how following the Bible's instructions to build a person up can help that person feel good about him- or herself. Now let's plan a specific way we can build someone up this week.**

CONCLUSION (3-5 minutes)

Materials needed: Post-it Notes or index cards, pencils.

Have each student work privately to think of a specific person they can build up this week. The person can be someone their age, a neighbor or a family member. Suggest that students choose persons they would not normally be inclined to build up. Direct each student to write on a Post-it Note or index card a compliment or encouragement he or she could say to the person. The note or card can be placed in his or her Bible, purse or wallet as a reminder to build that person up. Encourage each student to be sincere in his or her compliment and to observe the response of the person complimented. Say, **Also make note of how building that person up makes you feel about yourself.**

Close in audible prayer asking God to remind your students to watch their words and use opportunities to build others up

INTEGRITY

DEWEY BERTOLINI

KEY VERSES

"Lord, who may dwell in your sanctuary? Who may live on your holy hill? He whose walk is blameless and who does what is righteous, who speaks the truth from his heart." Psalm 15:1,2

BIBLICAL BASIS

Genesis 2:16,17; 3:6,22-24; 6:11-22; 26:7; Exodus 23:2; Numbers 13:1,2,26—14:4,34; 16:1-3,28-34; Joshua 7:1,20-26; 1 Samuel 18:6-9; 2 Samuel 11:2-5,14,15; 12:11-18; 2 Kings 5:14-27; Psalm 10:4; Proverbs 18:12; Matthew 27:3-5; Luke 23:20-25; Acts 5:1-11; Romans 5:12-14; James 3:16; 1 John 1:9

FOCUS OF THE SESSION

A commitment to personal integrity among Christians will have a great impact for the cause of Christ in our world.

AIMS OF THIS SESSION

You and your students will have accomplished the purpose of this Bible study session if you can:

- EXAMINE the examples of Bible characters and IDENTIFY the consequences that compromising or maintaining their integrity had in their situations;
- DISCUSS reasons people compromise their integrity;
- WRITE a description of an area where you have compromised your integrity and PRAY, confessing that area to God and asking Him to restore your integrity.

TEACHER'S BIBLE STUDY

"Everything you say sounds so nice, but Christianity simply does not work."

Jim blurted out his words in an angry response to a message I had just given at Hume Lake Christian Camps conference center. Upon examining the evidence, Jim had made up his mind and would consider no other options. Christianity constituted a 2,000-year-old fraud. No one could persuade him otherwise.

I can't blame him for feeling this way. Consider the facts. Jim grew up in a pastor's home—that is, until his father landed in jail after raping a 16-year-old girl. Upon his release on parole, Jim's dad started using his son as a personal punching bag.

"You have no idea what I face at home," Jim exclaimed. "I'm scared to death of the man. And you want me to commit my life to the same Jesus my dad preached about? No way! Don't you understand? Christianity just doesn't work."

Explaining the Problem

Christianity has degenerated worldwide and is suffering from a gargantuan credibility crisis. The decade of the 80s has taken its toll—and I'm not talking about the headline scandals that rocked the Church during the latter part of the decade. I am referring to the daily scandals that decimate our corporate credibility on an ongoing basis.

Perhaps a few examples will serve to illustrate this fact:

A friend of mine hired a Christian contractor to do a room addition for $7,000. Upon completion of the project, my friend received a bill for nearly $14,000. My friend's comment to me? "I will never hire a Christian again."

A realtor friend of mine told me that he works with several Christians in his office. "I cannot trust a single one of them," he lamented. "If I told you about their unethical business practices, you wouldn't believe me."

As a girls' softball coach, I have established friendships with several of the umpires in our city. Do you know what they told me? "When we work church league games, we are subjected to more harassment and profanity than during industrial league games."

My sister works as a waitress at a prominent restaurant in town. She recently admitted, "I hate Sunday nights. That's when the church crowd comes in. They complain more regularly, send their food back with greater frequency and leave the smallest tips of anyone."

One of my students just returned to school after spending her summer as a hostess for a rather ritzy hotel. When I asked her about her opportunities to witness to her colleagues, she gave me a cynical laugh. "Are you kidding? They hate the Christian groups with a passion. The Christians bickered and griped and left their rooms in messier conditions than any other group."

I wish I had a dollar for every girl who has told me that the unsaved guys she dates treat her with greater respect than the Christian guys.

While substitute teaching at a high school in my area, I began talking to several of the regular teachers. One of them asked me, "Why do my Christian students cut class and cheat on their exams just as much as my other students?"

Contemporary Compromise

Our corporate credibility has landed upon some hard times. I bemoaned this fact as I stood before over 1,600 students during chapel at a prominent Christian university. I asked them to raise their hands if they could answer yes to any of these questions:

- How many of you have a Christian friend who is currently involved in an immoral sexual relationship?
- Have any of these resulted in an unwanted pregnancy?
- Have any of these ended in an abortion?

- How many of you have a Christian friend who abuses alcohol?
- How about a Christian friend who uses illegal drugs?
- Have any of them become addicted?
- How about Christian friends who cheat on their schoolwork?
- How about a Christian friend who has stolen someone else's property?
- How many of you know of Christian marriages that have ended in divorce?

Needless to say, in response to *every* question, hands went up throughout the auditorium. My words that followed shocked some of the students into the raw reality of our contemporary state of compromise: "I have been a Christian for 21 years. I know what I believe and why I believe it. But if today I was a non-Christian searching for the truth, based upon your raised hands I would reject Christianity as a fraud. No other intellectually honest conclusion could be drawn. Talk is cheap, men and women. If Christianity doesn't work to keep us out of bed with one another, out of abortion clinics, off of drugs or out of divorce court, then Christianity simply does not work."

Christianity has degenerated worldwide and is suffering from a gargantuan credibility crisis.

Returning to a commitment to personal integrity has become for Christians the compelling issue of the 1990s. In his thought-provoking book, *The Frog in the Kettle*, George Barna includes in his imperative to the church these challenging words.

To the average nonbeliever, Christians act no differently than anyone else. Our faith appears to be simply a theoretical construct, an emotional decision that does not have the power to transform who we are and how we behave. During the '90s, we must forcefully demonstrate, through our actions, that what we believe dictates what we do....Christians should be discernible as people of integrity and love.[1]

"Integrity." I looked up this word in a variety of dictionaries and found a variety of definitions. By distilling them into one workable thought, I arrived at the following definition: "Integrity gives us the ability to stand in front of any group of people, anywhere, any time, allow them to ask us anything they want about our private lives and answer every question honestly without being ashamed." Nothing hidden. Nothing buried. Integrity is a commitment to basic honesty.

Integrity does not imply perfection, but rather a life orientation of pursuing purity and righteousness. If Christians like you and I would live our lives by this definition, I am convinced that the corporate credibility of Christians would be restored.

A Study in Contrasts

Joseph was an individual whose life story stands in stark contrast to the compromises I previously described. As illustrated in Genesis 39, Joseph had a motive for compromising his integrity and an opportunity to do so. And yet, under the heat of temptation, Joseph stood firm and true as a man of unquestioned integrity.

Motive: Joseph experienced indescribable rejection as his 11 brothers sold him into slavery. Can you even begin to imagine the indignity he must have felt as his brothers watched the slave traders shackle him and drag him off into bondage? He was forced to live in a foreign country away from family and friends, and in an unfamiliar culture surrounded by strange customs and a difficult language. Joseph must have felt loneliness settle upon him like a dark, dank fog of doom.

Opportunity: When Joseph arrived in Egypt he was sold into the service of Potiphar, one of Pharaoh's officials. While in Potiphar's home Joseph prospered and was given much responsibility and freedom. Potiphar's lascivious wife set her eyes upon the young and virile Joseph. While away on business, Potiphar left Joseph in charge of the household—the perfect set-up for Mrs. Potiphar to raise the heat and for Joseph to compromise his integrity without being caught in the act.

The key to understanding the pressure Joseph experienced comes in the form of a short, three-word phrase: "day after day" (Gen. 39:10). Joseph did not experience a one-time seduction. Mrs. Potiphar pursued him day after day in a relentless attempt to erode his convictions. Joseph did not budge.

Finally, in a last-ditch effort to conquer her prey, Mrs. Potiphar grabbed Joseph by his coat and tried to forcibly rape him. "Come to bed with me!" she demanded (v. 12). "But he left his cloak in her hand and ran out of the house" (v. 12).

> Integrity does not imply perfection, but rather a life orientation of pursuing purity and righteousness.

What did Joseph get in return? Did they put his picture on the cover of *People* magazine and herald him as a pillar of virtue in a decadent land? No way. Mrs. Potiphar falsely accused Joseph of attempted rape and had him thrown into a dungeon (see vv. 16-20).

This story teaches an important lesson: We do not do what is right simply because of all of the goodies we might get in return. We do what is right simply because it is right and what God requires—even if it lands us in a jail cell!

The Anatomy of Integrity

Before running from Mrs. Potiphar, Joseph made three significant statements that support the cause of uncompromised integrity. These declarations serve as a blueprint for you and me to keep our integrity intact.

First, Joseph stated, "My master has withheld nothing from me except you, because you are his wife" (v. 9). In other words, Joseph was saying, "If I go to bed with you, I violate my master." Do you realize that when you compromise your integrity you violate those who know you? How many people would you take down with you if you caved in to the pressure to compromise? How many people would call Christianity into question as a result? To what degree do you think these individuals would feel pain and disillusionment upon hearing the news that you fell?

Joseph's second statement is also revealing: "How then could I do such a wicked thing?" (v. 9). With the emphasis upon the pronoun "I," Joseph in effect said, "If I go to bed with you, I violate myself." No pain can compare to the agony of looking into a mirror and seeing the reflection of a hypocrite. The consequences of sin have a way of catching up with us, exposing us and destroying our self-esteem. On the other hand, nothing can compare with living with a clear conscience before God and others—even when our circumstances are difficult as a result.

Joseph finished his second statement with four important words: "and sin against God" (v. 9)? In essence Joseph was saying, "If I go to bed with you, Mrs. Potiphar, I violate God." Unthinkable. Unconscionable. Inconceivable. How dare we, through such a selfish choice, violate the one who died for us, shed His blood for us, went to the tomb for us, rose from the dead for us and now lives to give our lives meaning and purpose? When we violate our integrity, by whatever means, we injure our relationship with God and handicap our ability to respond to His voice and enjoy His presence.

Some Great News!

Have you blown your integrity? Can you pinpoint areas of compromise in your own life? If so, then do I have some great news for you: Your integrity can be restored. "How?" you ask. First John 1:9 holds the answer: "If we confess our sins, he is faithful and just and will forgive us our sins and purify us from all unrighteousness."

The word "confess" has a very specific meaning: To say the same thing about our sin that God says. God says three things about sin: (1) "I hate it" (see Ps. 5:4-6); (2) "It breaks my heart" (see Ps. 78:38-40); (3) "Don't do it again" (see John 8:11). When we transparently face the areas of compromise in our lives with this kind of honesty, God purifies us from all unrighteousness. Through confession and repentance we can start over with a clean slate before God and a clear conscience. Our integrity can be restored and we can begin the process of earning back the trust of others who have suffered because of our sin.

> **When we violate our integrity, by whatever means, we injure our relationship with God and handicap our ability to respond to His voice and enjoy His presence.**

Note
1. George Barna, *The Frog in the Kettle: What Christians Need to Know About Life in the Year 2000* (Ventura, CA: Regal Books, 1990), pp. 227, 228.

TEACHING PLAN

APPROACH (3-5 minutes)

Materials needed: Three or four articles from a current newspaper that describe actions that violate God's commands.

Introduce this session by showing and summarizing the content of the newspaper articles you have selected. Ask the students to suggest possible consequences that may have resulted because the person (people) involved compromised their integrity.

Move to the Bible Exploration by saying, **Compromising integrity is nothing new in our world. As you can see, it happens every day. Such behavior from unsaved people, although wrong, is not uncommon or unexpected. But what happens when Christians compromise their integrity?**

ALTERNATE APPROACH (5-7 minutes)

Use this Alternate Approach instead of the Approach above if you feel it best suits the needs and interests of the students in your class.

Materials needed: Chalkboard and chalk or newsprint and felt pen, scratch paper, pencils.

Begin this session by asking students to raise their hands if they can answer yes to the following question: How many of you have a friend or family member who has rejected Jesus Christ as the only true Lord and Savior? Move the class into groups of three or four and distribute scratch paper and pencils. Have the students work in their groups to list as many reasons as they can for why someone might reject Christ.

After a few minutes, gather the student's attention and ask them to share their reasons. Compile a summary of their reasons on the board or newsprint. Make certain that the reason "because of all the hypocrites in the churches" is included in your summary list. As needed, define the meaning of hypocrite. As a class, use numbers to prioritize the reasons on the list from the most common, serious reason to the least significant.

Move to the Bible Exploration by saying, **The "hypocrite excuse" is considered by many to be an insignificant reason for rejecting Jesus Christ. But in a world where integrity is so easily compromised, hypocrisy among those who call themselves "Christians" should be seen as a significant reason why people often reject Jesus Christ. Today we are going to look at what integrity is and the impact compromising our integrity can have.**

BIBLE EXPLORATION (35-45 minutes)

Materials needed: Bibles, a copy for each student of the "Consequences of Compromise" student worksheet, Post-it Notes, scratch paper, pencils, chalkboard and chalk or newsprint and felt pen. Optional—a copy for each student of the "Keeping Integrity Intact" student worksheet (see the Alternate Step 2).

Preparation: On five Post-it Notes write the following verse references—one group of references per note (see Step 3): Luke 23:20-25 and Exodus 23:2; 1 Samuel 18:6-9; Psalm 10:4 and Proverbs 18:12; Genesis 26:7;

James 3:16. As students arrive distribute the Post-its and ask the recipients to be prepared to read aloud their assigned verses when you indicate.

Step 1 (5-6 minutes)
As a class, compile a list of situations you know of in which someone was hurt because a Christian compromised his or her integrity. (As necessary, suggest situations listed in the "Explaining the Problem" section of the Teacher's Bible Study.) Review your list and then work together to define what it means to compromise integrity.

Optional—instead of compiling a list, ask the students to respond to the series of questions listed in the "Contemporary Compromise" section of the Teacher's Bible Study. Then work together to define what it means to compromise integrity.

Step 2 (10-12 minutes)
Point out that for every breach of integrity, consequences result. Say, **Let's look at several Bible peoples' lives and see the impact compromising their integrity had.** Move the students into groups of three to four and distribute pencils and copies of the "Consequences of Compromise" student worksheet. Instruct the group members to work together to complete the sheet.

After about ten minutes gather the students' attention and briefly review their answers to the sheet (following are the correct answers).

- Achan stole gold, silver and a beautiful robe; he and his family were stoned to death.
- Ananias and Sapphira lied to God; they were struck dead.
- Gehazi collected payment from a man for God's miraculous healing; he contracted leprosy.
- Adam and Eve disobeyed God in spite of His warning of death; they brought sin and death to the whole human race.
- Ten spies and the Israelites doubted God's ability to give Israel their promised land; they wandered in the wilderness for 40 years.
- David committed adultery and murder; his child died.
- Korah rebelled against Moses' God-given authority; the ground opened and swallowed him, his family and his men.
- Judas betrayed Jesus Christ for 30 pieces of silver; he committed suicide.

Alternate Step 2 (10-12 minutes)
Complete this alternate step instead of Step 2 above if

you want to approach the topic of integrity from a more positive point of view.

Move the students into groups of three to four and distribute the "Keeping Integrity Intact" student worksheet and pencils. Say, **Work with your group to identify each person who kept their integrity intact. For each person's situation, write something positive that resulted from their unwillingness to compromise their integrity.** After about eight minutes, gather the students' attention and briefly review their answers to the sheet (following are the correct answers).

1. Result: Jesus made salvation available to the entire world.
2. Result: Through Noah's obedience the human race was preserved when God judged humankind's wickedness by sending a flood over the earth.
3. Result: Elijah's uncompromising example of faith turned the people toward God.
4. Result: Peter and John's example encouraged other believers to boldly proclaim the truth about Jesus.
5. Result: God was with Shadrach, Meshach and Abednego, protected them from the fire and caused the king of Babylon to praise and honor God.
6. Result: God was with Joseph and allowed him to prosper even though he was in prison. (Briefly describe Joseph's circumstances and how God used them to preserve an entire nation during a time of famine—see Gen. 45:4-11).

Step 3 (10-12 minutes)
Ask the students to think about the following question: **If maintaining integrity is important and compromising it often has severe consequences, why do you think people violate their integrity?** Then ask the volunteers to whom you gave Post-its to to read their verses (see the Preparation). After each verse is read, ask a volunteer to share a reason the verse gives why a person might compromise his or her integrity. Compile their reasons into a list on the board or newsprint.

When all the verses have been shared, discuss the following questions: **What other reason's would you add to this list? What reasons do kids your age give for doing what is wrong? What effect would the compromise of a Christian friend have on you? On your relationship with God and other Christians? On how you relate to non-Christians you know?**

The following is a list of the verses and the reasons these verses give for why people compromise their integrity.

- Luke 23:20-25 and Exodus 23:2: Peer pressure; Because of the pressure from the crowd, Pilate compromised even though he knew Jesus was innocent.

- 1 Samuel 18:6-9: Anger and feelings of revenge; Saul wanted to hurt David because of feelings of anger and jealousy.
- Psalm 10:4 and Proverbs 18:12: Pride.
- Genesis 26:7: Fear. Out of fear of what others would do, Isaac lied.
- James 3:16: Envy and selfishness.

Step 4 (10-15 minutes)

Read aloud the following quote from George Barna's book, *The Frog in the Kettle:*

To the average nonbeliever, Christians act no differently than anyone else. Our faith appears to be simply a theoretical construct, an emotional decision that does not have the power to transform who we are and how we behave. During the '90s, we must forcefully demonstrate, through our actions, that what we believe dictates what we do....Christians should be discernible as people of integrity and love.

Direct your students to return to their groups of three to four. On scratch paper (or the back of a worksheet) have each group plan ways members of their group can respond to someone who has rejected or is critical of Christianity because of the compromises of Christians. Ask them to decide what they could *say* and *do* to demonstrate by their integrity their faith to other kids their age. As needed, refer the students to Joseph's example of integrity given in Genesis 39.

Allow eight to ten minutes for the groups to work. Then ask several volunteers to share their groups' ideas. Ask, **What do you think would result if all Christians kept their integrity intact?**

Move to the Conclusion by saying, **It is difficult for us to make changes in our individual lives and earn back the respect of those who may have suffered because of our compromises of integrity. Let's look at what we can and need to do to restore our integrity and be an example of Christ to others.**

CONCLUSION (3-5 minutes)

Materials needed: Bibles, 3x5-inch index cards, pencils. Optional—a copy of the booklet, *So, What's a Christian Anyway?* (published by Gospel Light Publications, see p. 127).

Ask the students to follow in their Bibles as you read aloud 1 John 1:9. Say, **This verse explains in a nutshell how we can have our integrity restored when we blow it—even if we've made big compromises in our lives.** Ask, **What does this verse say we need to do to have our integrity restored? What does this verse say God will do if we confess our sins?** Briefly discuss the meaning of this verse as it applies to individual lives. As needed refer to the material in the "Some Great News!" section of the Teacher's Bible Study.

Say, **Everyone is vulnerable to sin and compromise. The Bible says that "all have sinned and fall short of the glory of God"** (Rom. 3:23). **Because of this, we all need to have our integrity restored. We all need to ask for God's help and work daily in cooperation with Him to keep our integrity intact.** (You may want to refer to Ps. 32:8-10 and Rom. 12:1,2.)

Distribute index cards and pencils to the students. Have each student write on his or her card an area of compromise where he or she would like to have integrity restored. Lead the class in a prayer of confession, claiming God's complete forgiveness for those who desire to have their integrity restored.

Announce to the class that when confession has taken place, God restores a person's integrity. It is now each person's responsibility to work with God's help to maintain their integrity. It is also each person's responsibility to rebuild the trust of those who have suffered because of their compromise. To symbolize the restoration of their integrity, you may direct the students to tear up their index cards.

After this session, be available to any students who want to talk with you. If questions concerning God's willingness to forgive sin arise, you may want to use the "How to Become a Christian" section of the booklet *So, What's a Christian Anyway?* to present God's plan for forgiveness and salvation. Also see the article titled "Presenting Christ to Young People" on p. 12 of this teacher's manual.

WHEN PARENTS ARE SUBSTANCE ABUSERS

DOUG WEBSTER

KEY VERSE

"My Father, who has given them to me, is greater than all; no one can snatch them out of my Father's hand." John 10:29

BIBLICAL BASIS

Deuteronomy 5:16; 6:6,7; 27:16; Proverbs 20:1; 23:22; John 10:27-29; Acts 5:27-29; 1 Corinthians 6:19,20; 12:24b-26; Ephesians 4:29-32; 5:18; 6:1-4; Colossians 3:13,20,21; 1 Thessalonians 2:11,12

FOCUS OF THE SESSION

Through the support of the Body of Christ, our heavenly Father provides the person with a substance-abusing parent the opportunity to be part of a healthy, whole family.

AIMS OF THIS SESSION

You and your students will have accomplished the purpose of this Bible study session if you can:
- EXAMINE in Scripture God's model for a healthy, functioning family;
- DISCUSS the impact a substance-abusing parent can have on the health of his or her family;
- IDENTIFY ways to deal with parents who are substance abusers.

TEACHER'S BIBLE STUDY

I had just finished speaking to a group about drugs and personal chemical warfare. I stood in the church's sanctuary answering questions from a crowd composed of both parents and students. The usual questions came up: "What can I do if my kid's on drugs?" "How can I keep them from using drugs?" "What about my son's friends? I can't control them."

Then the zinger came. A young man in his late teens said, "What do you do if your parents are the abusers in the family?"

So much attention concerning today's problems with drugs and alcohol is placed on young people. The young man's question opened up the very real and powerful issue of parental substance abuse.

As youth workers sharing God's Word with students, it is crucial that we understand and deal with the influence of the family on each member of our groups. For all our hard work, we need to realize that the one hour we spend with students in a Bible study or youth group meeting is very limited compared to the hours upon hours each student spends under the influence, values and life-style of his or her family. If a student's home atmosphere does not support the spiritual truths we are trying to teach, we need to be sensitive to the confusion and tension that student is probably experiencing.

Living in a family where a parent abuses drugs, alcohol or some other substance is very much a possibility for some of your students. The topic of drug and alcohol abuse is not new to your students, but learning to develop healthy coping methods to deal with a substance-abusing parent often is. Your students need practical resources to find hope and help for such a crisis situation—whether it be in their own home or that of a friend or family member.

A Common Scenario

"At least we don't have a problem in my group. They're all such good kids." Have you heard that before? Have you thought that before? Some members of youth groups are "good kids." They believe in right and wrong. Some do so because they have received a foundation of faith from their parents that they are now beginning to live out for themselves. Other students attend youth groups because of their desire to make things better, right, good. That's not all bad. But some seek the good because they come from families that are led by parents who have serious problems with drugs and alcohol and the students are trying to make up for the lack of esteem they receive at home.

This second situation is typical of a dysfunctional family. The family is out of balance. Like a teeter-totter with three on one side and only one on the other, the family does not work correctly.

Often a dysfunctional family will produce one child who takes on the responsibility of making the family function correctly. They are responsible "good" kids like some of the kids you may have in your group. They make great student leaders. You can rely on them. Why? They have learned at a young age that Mom or Dad, or both, will not take care of the family because of their problem. So they compensate for their parents' inability.

If the child lets the abusing parent face the consequences of their drug or alcohol problem without trying to act as a buffer, the child often receives abuse from the parent. The parent may abuse the child verbally, physically and even sexually. It is not uncommon for such a parent to move from drug abuse to one form or another of child abuse. Because of this, the child will probably fear seeking change. He or she may think, "I'd rather have my parent abuse substances than abuse me." Even

with the protective measures the child takes, more often than not abuse is directed at him or her anyway.

This type of family makes me think of a young girl in my past youth group. I'll call her Linda. Linda was 15 and very mature when I met her. She got good grades. Even an A minus grade was not good enough for her. She had a job at an early age. Linda played on a couple of sports teams and did well. On top of all this she was friendly, pretty and well-liked. She started coming to our group because of a friend, but she managed to stay plugged in long after the friend left. Linda attached herself to the moral fiber of Christianity. It seemed so natural for her. What made Linda seem so exceptional in comparison to many of her peers?

I discovered the answer when I met her mom. Linda's mom was in and out of jobs. She was going to school a little bit and working here and there. Most of her spending (extravagant as it was) came from the child and alimony support her ex-husband gave to her. Linda's mom was an alcoholic. She was explosive with her anger and she made big ordeals out of Linda's simple problems so common to adolescence. She despised Linda's boyfriend, but when Linda broke up with him and started dating another guy, Linda's mom thought the first boyfriend was great.

> **The topic of drug and alcohol abuse is not new to your students, but learning to develop healthy coping methods to deal with a substance-abusing parent often is.**

What was happening? The impact of Linda's relationship with her mom was shaping Linda into a dysfunctional person, even though Linda's habits seemed so "good." Linda, in my opinion, had become the parent of the family because Mom was not coping with life. Mom chose to drink. Linda chose to be the parent.

When a Family Doesn't Function

It's amazing how families develop common patterns when they quit working correctly. Like actors in a movie, each family member plays a particular part or combination of different roles.

The abusing parent fills the role of the *addict*. His or her problem dominates the family.

Often the other parent (and/or a child—especially in single parent families) takes on the role of the *enabler* or *co-dependent*. The enabler actually perpetuates the abuse by covering up for the abuser or clean-

60

ing up the messes or problems made by the abuser.

Other family members also take on various roles. The *scapegoat* receives much of the blame for the family's problems; the *loner* disappears or withdraws from the family; the *clown* makes a joke of everything, trying to distract the family from the real problem; the *hero* is the good kid who tries to save the family name by getting the good grades or never settling for anything short of perfection.

These families lose their ability to trust each other, to communicate their feelings and to address the source of their dysfunction. In short, they simply quit working.

Substance abuse in a family can be compared to having an elephant in the living room. How the family responds to the elephant shows whether the family is functional or dysfunctional. In a functional, balanced family, you'd hear responses such as: "Mom, come quick! There's an elephant in the room." "Oh no, how are we going to clean up after this animal?" "Call the zoo. We need help. It's too big for us to handle."

On the other hand, a family out of balance may not express a response at all. The family cleans up after the elephant and acts like the problem doesn't exist. An enabling spouse may say something like, "Well, you know, things like this happen all the time. I'm sure it will leave soon." Heroes in the family try to ride the elephant or do acrobatics in another part of the house to gain the approval of the family. Clowns may make fun of the elephant to distract the family.

There are two outcomes to such a situation: either somebody will do something about the elephant or the elephant will destroy the house and family. Unchecked substance abuse in a family is like having a live-in elephant in the house.

God's Original Design

In His Word, God has created a healthy model of how a family is supposed to function. It is important that your students understand how this model works so they can lay a foundation for building a healthy family of their own someday—whether or not their current family situation has slipped from God's original intention.

In a nutshell, God's Word prescribes that for a family to function according to His design, children should obey their parents and parents should be sensitive and fair in dealing with and disciplining their children (see Eph.

> **Substance abuse in a family can be compared to having an elephant in the living room.**

6:1-4; Col. 3:20,21). The motivation for both the parents and the children to build a healthy, functioning family centers around individual allegiance to the Lord and a desire to live in peace with each other.

Studying what God's Word says about this topic will benefit all the students in your class—not just those who are in crisis family situations. For those from healthy families, the purpose of this study will be preventing a future crisis and enabling them to support friends and family who are grappling with substance abuse. Rather than waiting for a crisis to happen before searching the mind and heart of God, you will be helping your students put the Lord at the center of the prevention process. By learning God's design for a family, they will be building safeguards for future crises in their present families or future families.

This study also serves the purpose of providing real, practical help for students who are part of a family that has slipped from God's original design. If these students are Christians, the obligation to obey a parent becomes complicated when the parent abuses substances. According to Scripture, substance abuse is wrong (see Prov. 20:1; 1 Cor. 6:19,20; Eph. 5:18)—and a parent who abuses substances is rarely able to fulfill God's prescribed role as a parent. As a youth worker, how do you respond to the needs of these kids?

Consider the situation of Linda whom I described earlier. Would you advise Linda to abandon her mom and her role as her mom's daughter? Can you encourage Linda to obey her mom without encouraging her to support her mom's substance abuse? Are there ever times when you should guide a student to disobey a parent? What practical suggestions and support can you give the Lindas in your youth group?

There are no easy answers to these questions, but there are answers. First, according to God's command it is your students' obligation to obey their parents. Second, it is your students' obligation to put God and His desires first (see Acts 4:18-20; 5:25-29). When what God desires conflicts with what a parent requires of his or her child, the child must obey God. Judging such a situation is difficult—especially for a teenager who is just beginning to learn to make mature decisions about life and faith. Your role as a youth worker can have a significant impact in this area and that impact should be weighed carefully.

One significant word of comfort you can give students who live with substance-abusing parents is that, where their parents fail, God does not. Those who place their faith in Christ have the support of a heavenly Father and a greater earthly family. These kids need to know that whatever situation they are in, Father God is big enough to help them deal with it. Jesus addresses this by describing the security members of His family enjoy: "My sheep listen to my voice; I know them, and they follow me. I give them eternal life, and they shall never perish; no one can snatch them out of my hand. My Father, who has given them to me, is greater than all; no one can snatch them out of my Father's hand" (John 10:27-29).

The primary element to successfully coping with a substance abusing parent and dysfunctional home situation is faith in Christ. Through faith, a teenager in a dysfunctional family can combat the negative influences in his or her home, share in promoting healing if possible and learn to establish his or her own family in a manner that is healthy and according to God's design.

> **One significant word of comfort you can give students who live with substance-abusing parents is that, where their parents fail, God does not.**

If the family as a unit turns to Christ and faces its problems, it can experience grace and forgiveness—two important ingredients for the process of recovery from dysfunction. It is interesting to note that virtually every recovery treatment plan for addiction implemented in our society acknowledges God (or makes reference to a Supreme Being) as an integral part of the recovery process. Discovering God's grace frees family members to receive and dispense forgiveness. Forgiveness empowers an abuser and his or her family members to heal into a functioning family.

A second element that will help students deal with a substance abusing parent is the family of God. Once a person is planted in Christ, he or she can rest in the support of this greater, healthier family. Where his or her family may fail, God's family can step in. In spite of the circumstances in their biological families, students with substance-abusing parents can be healthy, whole people and enjoy the benefits of a healthy, whole family. It is the responsibility of each member of God's family to see that hurting members are supported and encouraged.

A Final Note of Caution

Dealing with the topic of parents who are substance abusers is touchy and complicated. I do not recommend that you send your group of high schoolers out the door on a hunt for drug-abusing parents. You may uncover more problems than you are ready to handle. I also do not recommend that you use your teaching time to hold group therapy for those who are struggling with this issue.

I do recommend that you schedule time after this study for the students to share their personal situations with you, a pastor or a Christian counselor trained in the area of substance abuse. You may also want to compile and make available book and video resources for families wanting more help and education on the issues of substance abuse and recovery. Be ready to recommend a reputable Christian treatment center to which you can refer students and their families.

Pray that the Holy Spirit will provide your students with the love, forgiveness and courage they need to deal with their home situations according to God's will. Don't feel that as a teacher you need to be the expert on substance abuse. Know your limitations and rally the appropriate support your students and their families need to find healing and to help others cope with and overcome substance abuse.

Note: For more information about substance abuse and the specific effects it can have on an individual, see the teacher's manual and paperback book titled *Hot Buttons I* (published by Gospel Light Publications, 1986).

You may also want to include the following books in your library.

Arterburn, Stephen. *Growing Up Addicted.* New York: Ballantine Books, Inc., 1989.

Arterburn, Stephen and Burns, Jim. *Drug-Proof Your Kids:...And Help Them Say No.* Pomona, CA: Focus on the Family Publishing, 1989.

Beattie, Melody. *Codependent No More: How to Stop Controlling Others and Start Caring for Yourself.* Center City, MN: Hazelden Foundation, 1987.

Burns, Jim. *Surviving Adolescence: Or Growing Up Oughta Be Easier Than This.* Waco, TX: Word Books, 1990.

Burns, Jim. *The Youth Worker's Book of Case Studies.* Ventura, CA: Gospel Light Publications, 1987.

TEACHING PLAN

APPROACH (5-7 minutes)

Materials needed: Chalkboard and chalk or felt pen and newsprint.

Describe for the group the following situation.

Larry is a Christian and a junior in high school. Returning home from a date, Larry walks in and finds his dad lying naked and passed out on the floor. His dad is drunk—*again*. If you were Larry, how would you feel? What would you do in this situation?

List the students' responses to the situation on the board or newsprint. Include at least five actions Larry could take to deal with the situation. Ask the members of the group to vote on the one option that they feel is the best response. Circle that option, then ask, **What might be the consequences of making this choice?** List the group's ideas. Ask, **What if this situation happened all the time? How would this change your response?**

After a few moments of discussion, move to the Exploration by saying, **Today we're going to talk about parents who are substance abusers and how teenagers can deal with this kind of home situation—whether it is in their immediate family or that of a friend or relative.**

BIBLE EXPLORATION (40-50 minutes)

Materials needed: Bibles, a copy for each student of the "God's Design for Families" student worksheet, pencils, chalkboard and chalk or newsprint and felt pen.

Preparation: Letter the following question on the chalkboard or newsprint: "What do these verses tell you about God and those who belong to Him?" (see Step 4).

Step 1 (5-8 minutes)

Use the following illustration to describe what happens when a parent abuses substances and the family ceases to function correctly. Choose five volunteers from the group—two girls and three guys—to help you. Each volunteer will represent a member of a dysfunctional family. As you introduce and describe each member, pose him or her according to their role in the family.

Identify a male volunteer as the father of the family. Bend him over at the waist. Say, **This is Dad. Because of the stresses and strains of life, he chooses to drink away his sorrows. He drinks a lot and often. He has lost three jobs because of his drinking. He's an alcoholic, or the *addict* of the family. Of course this could be the mom just as well, but we chose the dad.**

Identify a female volunteer as the mother of the family. Place her on her knees next to Dad. Say, **This is Mom. She keeps the house clean and tries to cover up every problem or mess Dad makes. She says things like, "Oh, honey, you really don't drink *that* much." Or, "I know life has been pretty tough lately...." She's been** saying things like this for the past eight years. She is an *enabler* or *co-dependent*.

Identify the other female volunteer as the oldest daughter and place her next to Mom. Instruct the daughter to display a big smile. Say, **This is the oldest sister. She is the *hero* of the family. She strives to get a 4.0 grade point average or better. She's always trying to be perfect. She pretends she doesn't notice Dad's problem. She even works full time after school trying to make up for Dad's lost jobs. She feels happiest when Mom and Dad are pleased with her performance.**

Identify another male volunteer as the middle son. Place him with his back to the family and standing off to one side. Say, **This is the middle kid. He's always doing something wrong. He takes drugs, ditches school and plays heavy metal music. You can bet that if there is yelling in the house, it's either about him or with him. He's the *scapegoat*. When he's not in trouble, he is hiding out somewhere—a real loner.**

Identify the last male volunteer as the youngest child. Sit him down and instruct him to make a funny face. Say, **This is junior. He's the youngest and by far the funniest. He's the family *clown*. He is the only one who can get Dad to laugh. When junior is not laughing, he's probably crying. He's a very moody kid.**

Summarize your illustration by saying, **This is an example of a family that is not functioning in the healthy way God designed families to operate. This is a common situation in families where one or both parents are substance abusers.**

Then move to Step 2 by saying, **Let's look at what God wants our families to be like and what we can do when our families slip from God's design.**

Step 2 (10-12 minutes)

Move the students into groups of four to six and distribute pencils and copies of the "God's Design for Families" student worksheet. Direct the members of each group to work together to complete the page.

After eight to ten minutes, gather the group members' attention and ask volunteers to share their responses to the questions on the page. Then say, **No one family perfectly fulfills what God prescribes a family to be like, and that is understandable. These verses serve as a model we can use to evaluate our families now and to strive for in the families we will be establishing in the future.**

Step 3 (12-15 minutes)

Introduce this step by saying, **When a family slips away from God's design as a result of substance abuse by a** parent, striving to do what God wants becomes difficult and confusing. Then lead a group discussion using the following verses and questions.

Ask volunteers to read aloud Proverbs 20:1, 1 Corinthians 6:19,20 and Ephesians 5:18. Ask, **How does God feel about substance abuse? How do you think substance abuse by a parent can affect his or her ability to fulfill God's design for a parent?** Encourage students to think of specific struggles a substance abusing parent may have, and areas where they may influence their families in ways that go against what God wants. You may want to list the students' ideas on the chalkboard or newsprint.

Then ask, **How can a son or daughter be obedient and respectful to a parent who is a substance abuser? Why do you think obedience is difficult in such a situation?** Ask a volunteer to read Acts 5:27-29. Explain that Peter and the apostles were told by the authorities not to talk about Jesus. Ask, **What reason did Peter and the apostles give for their disobedience? How do you think their experience applies to obeying parental authority? What limits do you think need to be placed on obeying a substance-abusing parent?**

Brainstorm specific situations that clearly illustrate putting obedience to God before obedience to a substance-abusing parent. Examples may include: not buying illegal drugs for the parent; removing him- or herself from verbal, physical or sexual abuse by the parent; not lying to cover for the parent. **How might appropriate obedience to that parent—whether or not the parent seems to deserve it—positively influence a son or daughter's home situation?**

Conclude this discussion by saying, **It is very difficult to judge when obedience to a parent is necessary and when it goes against God's design. In such cases it is wise to consult God's Word and ask for input from a mature Christian adult.**

Step 4 (3-5 minutes)

If you are a member of a family where a substance-abusing parent is present, you may feel that your situation is hopeless. You may see yourself taking on one of the roles common in a dysfunctional family. There are several ways you can find hope, help your situation and cultivate a healthy sense of family.

Direct the students to return to their groups of four to six, read John 10:27-29 and discuss the following question you have written on the chalkboard or newsprint (see the Preparation): "What do these verses tell you about God and those who belong to Him?"

After three to five minutes, ask a few volunteers to share from their groups' discussion. Follow up the students' responses by saying, **Whenever we face a crisis situation in our homes or elsewhere, it is vital that we realize we can rely on a heavenly Father who does not change and who is greater than our circumstances. No matter what happens to us or to life around us, those who belong to God can find the love and support that we need to make it in life.**

Read aloud 1 Corinthians 12:24b-26. Say, **Those who belong to God are members of His family. This family is often referred to in the Bible as the Body of Christ.** Then ask, **How can being a member of God's family help a son or daughter deal with having a parent who is a substance abuser?** Allow time for one or two students to respond.

Step 5 (10 minutes)

Introduce this step by saying, **Let's brainstorm some specific things kids your age can do to respond to a home situation where a substance-abusing parent is present. First let's list ideas that a teenager could use to help a friend who is in this situation.** Allow time for students to suggest several responses. Responses might include: praying with and for the friend; providing a place where the friend can stay if he or she is being abused at home; giving daily support and encouragement; offering to go with him or her to talk with an adult counselor or pastor about the situation.

Then say, **Now let's list ideas a teenager who is in this situation can use.** Take time to brainstorm at least five ideas. Here are some suggestions that you can include in your list.

- Establish a personal relationship with Christ and seek the support of a local body of believers.
- Adopt another family for emotional and perhaps physical support. **If you were in this situation, where could you find a family to provide the love and guidance you need to make it through?**
- Ask for wisdom and prayer from the pastor or a mature adult Christian.
- Study God's Word for help in making decisions about obeying a substance-abusing parent.
- Ask members of the church youth group to provide the support of brothers and sisters.
- Join a support group such as Alateen or Alanon.
- Seek the guidance of a professional counselor.

Conclude this step by saying, **Experts recommend that if you feel you have a problem with substance abuse in your own life or your family's, seek help.**

Most likely you're right. If you are not sure, I would be glad to talk with you about it after this study. If you do not choose to complete the Optional Step 6, move to the Conclusion.

Optional Step 6 (2-3 minutes)

Share the following information about how a parent's abuse of substances can have a direct effect on his or her children.

1. Children of substance-abusing parents can be greatly influenced by the parents' values and habits.

2. They may have a biological predisposition toward addiction. As unfair as it may seem, children of substance-abusing parents are personally very vulnerable to substance abuse. If the child follows in the same habits of subtance use as the parent, he or she will likely end up an addict.

3. They will have to clear some barriers in order to deal with their home situations. The biggest barrier is overcoming denial that a problem exists. Not recognizing that abuse is happening, and feeling guilty for the abuse, also play a large part in prolonging problems. By accepting God's grace and forgiveness, guilt and denial can be confronted and dealt with.

Facing the reality that there is a problem with substance abuse in your family and that it is affecting you as a person is the first step in becoming a healthy, whole person. Let's look at our personal situations and see how we can respond to the problem of parents who abuse substances.

CONCLUSION (5-8 minutes)

Materials needed: A copy for each student of the "Facing the Problem" student worksheet and the "Help!" resource page, pencils.

Preparation: Optional—photocopy the "Help!" resource page onto cardstock. Cut apart the cards, fold them along the dotted lines and set them aside on a table or other surface. Note: Customize the cards giving the names and numbers of organizations that you feel will best help the students in your group. We have listed a few numbers that you may want to consider.

Distribute pencils and copies of the "Facing the Problem" student worksheet. Say, **There are two assignments** listed on the page. If you live in a home situation with a parent who is a substance abuser, complete the first assignment. If you do not live in this kind of home situation, think of a friend or other family member who does and then complete the second assignment.

Allow three to five minutes for students to work and pray silently. (Note: Due to its sensitive nature, you may want to direct students to complete this sheet privately after class.) Close in audible prayer thanking God that He is big enough to help us handle any problem and that there is hope for overcoming the problems associated with having a parent who is a substance abuser.

Before students leave, distribute copies of the "Help!" resource page. Optional—if you copied the resource page onto cardstock and cut the cards on the page apart, direct students to take individual cards to keep or share with a friend.

Optional—you may want to take action as a class to address the problems experienced by teenagers who have substance-abusing parents. If so, set a time to meet with interested students and plan the action the group wants to take. The following is a list of ideas you may want to consider.

- Find or start a hot line for teenagers who live with substance-abusing parents. Plan ways to make this information available to teenagers in your church and community.
- Establish a program to train your students as peer counselors. (You may want to become involved in an existing program if one is available.)
- Visit a local Christian treatment center to learn more about substance abuse and recovery.
- Ask a recovering alcoholic to give a testimony at a youth group meeting.
- Create a pamphlet about substance abuse to distribute at your youth group or to teenagers in your community.
- Ask a substance-abuse counselor to speak to your youth group.
- Start a resource library in your church on the subject of substance abuse, recovery and dysfunctional families.
- Ask your pastor to speak on the topic of substance abuse.

PORNOGRAPHY

CONNIE NEAL

KEY VERSES

"So I tell you this, and insist on it in the Lord, that you must no longer live as the Gentiles do, in the futility of their thinking. They are darkened in their understanding and separated from the life of God because of the ignorance that is in them due to the hardening of their hearts. Having lost all sensitivity, they have given themselves over to sensuality so as to indulge in every kind of impurity, with a continual lust for more." Ephesians 4:17-19

BIBLICAL BASIS

Proverbs 4:23; Mark 7:21; Galatians 6:1; Ephesians 4:2,19,32; 5:11; Philippians 4:8; 2 Timothy 2:22; James 1:14,15,21; 5:16,19,20; 1 Peter 4:8; 2 Peter 2:19; 1 John 1:9

FOCUS OF THE SESSION

Repeated exposure to pornography affects a person's perception of sexual intimacy and his or her expectations for relationships.

AIMS OF THIS SESSION

You and your students will have accomplished the purpose of this Bible study session if you can:
- DISCUSS the downward progression the Bible and clinical evidence says exposure to pornography can affect in a person's life;
- EXAMINE ways pornography hurts not only those viewing it, but countless others;
- DECIDE where to draw the line concerning your personal exposure to pornographic material.

TEACHER'S BIBLE STUDY

Pornography is affecting the lives of your students. Youth in the Church are not exempt from the bombardment and lure of sexually explicit material in our culture. Even those who have not been directly exposed to pornography must deal with peers whose thoughts and actions are being shaped by pornography's vivid images.

As a teacher, you play a key role in combating the negative effects of pornography. According to the 1986 United States Attorney General's Commission on Pornography, "appropriate education is the real solution to the problem of pornography. Images in pornography affect attitudes and behavior, and images can also prevent behavior or cause different behavior. Positive messages can address love, marriage and sex in a wholesome manner, and may also specifically address pornography by discussing its dangers to individuals and to society."[1]

Defining Pornography

The word pornography comes from the Greek word meaning "whore-writing" or descriptions of the activities of whores. Pornography is the representation of sexually explicit behavior intended to arouse sexual excitement. Those who think of pornography as being characterized by the partial nudity of "men's magazines" are sadly mistaken.

The bulk of pornography is focused on sexual activity and less than 10 percent of the materials available even depict normal heterosexual activities between one man and one woman. The other 90 plus percent depict all forms of perversions including group sex, rape, incest, defecation, urination, mutilation, torture, sex with all varieties of animals, sadomasochistic activities, bondage, homosexuality, child molestation and even murder in so-called "snuff films."[2]

Considering the impressionable nature of adolescents and the sway of peer pressure, the fact that these warped images of human sexuality are being fed into the minds of countless young people is tremendously alarming.

In an effort to define illegal pornographic or obscene materials, the United States Supreme Court set forth a definition of obscenity.[3] The guidelines of the definition are:

- Whether the average person, applying contemporary community standards, would find that the work, taken as a whole, appeals to prurient interest. (This simply means that the material is intended to produce sexual stimulation.)
- Whether the work depicts or describes, in a patently offensive way, sexual conduct specifically defined by the applicable state law. (This refers to materials depicting or describing ultimate sexual acts: intercourse, masturbation, oral sex, excretion, ejaculation.)
- Whether the work, taken as a whole, lacks serious literary, artistic, political or scientific value. (This excludes depictions or descriptions of sex that have a bona fide purpose unrelated to its possible titillating effect.)

Although this definition is on the books and may be used in prosecuting offenders, it has little impact because pornography laws are not being enforced.[4] The exception to this could be a minute percentage of child pornography cases that reach the courts. The victimization of children in pornography is one arena where the Christian community is beginning to combat pornography through education and civic involvement.

The Facts About Pornography

The following uncomfortable facts are given to open your eyes and sensitize you to the realities this generation is facing.

The primary consumers of pornographic materials are male adolescents between the ages of 12 and 17, to whom this material is easily (even overwhelmingly) available.[5] There are more stores selling pornographic videos in the United States than there are McDonald's restaurants.[6] Access is also possible through bookstores in local malls (Walden Books, a division of K-Mart), convenience stores (7-11), cable TV, dial-a-porn telephone numbers and vending machines selling pornography within easy access of anyone with change. The pornography industry in America today is an $8-*billion*-a-year operation, 85-90 percent of which is run by "organized crime."[7]

We must also recognize that child molesters expose their victims to pornography to break down their victims' natural resistance. The United States Department of Justice stated in 1988 that one in three females and one in seven males will be sexually molested before the age of eighteen.[8] Many times the molesters are family members who continue to exert tremendous control over the lives of their victims and demand that secrecy be maintained. One result is that child molestation victims often place the blame and shame of abuse received on themselves.

Dr. Victor Cline, a clinical psychologist at the University of Utah, is one of the most respected researchers in the field of sexual abuse. He has found a near-universal four-step pattern exhibited by sex offenders. First, an addiction to pornography develops which draws the person back for more stimulation. Second, there is an escalation in the need for more sexually explicit and shocking material in order to get the same sexual stimulation as before. Third, there occurs over time a desensitization to the material's effect. What was at first considered gross or taboo becomes acceptable and, in a sense, legitimized in the mind. The person begins to believe that "everyone does it." Fourth, there is an increasing tendency to start acting out the sexual activities seen in pornography. What was first fantasy slides into reality.[9]

Pornography is at the root of many social problems which impact your students' world. Clinical studies by the FBI, researchers at major universities and clinical professionals conclude that exposure to pornography affects the sexual attitudes of all those exposed—men and women alike. This exposure results in a view of human sexuality which is degraded, harmful and increasingly dehumanized. Those exposed often display attitudes which are warped by what they have seen. They become

> **Considering the impressionable nature of adolescents and the sway of peer pressure, the fact that these warped images of human sexuality are being fed into the minds of countless young people is tremendously alarming.**

67

more tolerant of deviant sexual behavior, trivialize rape, have less compassion for the victims of sexually violent assaults and show marked sexual callousness.[10]

The repeated use of pornographic material can also result in addiction. Recent research by Dr. James L. McGaugh at the University of California in Irvine suggests that sexual arousal through the use of pornographic images has an actual physiological effect. "Dr. McGaugh's findings suggest that a person's memories of sexually arousing experiences get locked into the brain by the chemical epinephrine. Once there, the memories are difficult to forget. Thus, powerful sexual memories keep reappearing on his mind's memory screen, stimulating and arousing him."[11]

A final factor to keep in mind is that men and women are created by God to respond in very different ways to sexual stimulants. It is widely accepted that men tend to be sexually stimulated by visual images. Therefore they can be quickly attracted to pornographic materials which are visual in nature. Men are often drawn to the physical aspect of sexual involvement, regardless of whether love is involved. It has been said that men will tend to give love to get sex (whereas women will tend to give sex to get love). Men are by far the primary audience for pornographic materials because it appeals directly to the male tendency to be attracted to the visual exposure of the body (particularly the genitals) and overtly sexual acts. In pornography, little time is "wasted" on developing relationships or considering the emotional needs of the female partner. Sex becomes merely a physical act. This is more appealing to a male audience and is usually unattractive and degrading to women.

Women, on the other hand, are drawn into sexual arousal through emotional, romantic and relational stimulation. They are not usually sexually aroused by merely visual channels. This is why women are inclined toward "steamy" romance novels, soap operas and romance in the media rather than pornography. Pornography does not typically appeal to the emotional desires of women. Yet women *can* become addicted to pornography just as men can, but the initial use of pornography is usually tied to wanting to please a sexual partner.[12]

According to Dr. Jerry R. Kirk in his book, *Mind Polluters*, the end products of viewing violent pornography are similar for both men and women.[13] Women who

have been exposed to massive amounts of pornography often look at rape as a trivial offense. This is ironic in that women (and children) are, by and large, the predominant victims of pornography.

Christians and Pornography

The Bible addresses pornography by dealing with the issues of lust and lasciviousness—stirring up sexual passions which cannot be satisfied within God's laws of conduct and which lead to corruption.

Mark 7:21-23 describes the heart as the source of sexually immoral behavior: "For from within, out of men's hearts, come evil thoughts, sexual immorality, theft, murder, adultery, greed, malice, deceit, lewdness, envy, slander, arrogance and folly. All these evils come from inside and make a man 'unclean.'" Jesus also warns that "anyone who looks at a woman lustfully has already committed adultery with her in his heart" (Matt. 5:28). It is obvious that God is concerned with the state of our hearts and not just our outward actions. The repeated use of pornography can be interpreted as a symptom of heart-felt emotional and spiritual need.

Ephesians 4:17-19 describes the sexually addictive results that ungodly living and a heart hardened toward God can have: "So I tell you this, and insist on it in the Lord, that you must no longer live as the Gentiles do, in the futility of their thinking. They are darkened in their understanding and separated from the life of God because of the ignorance that is in them due to the hardening of their hearts. Having lost all sensitivity, they have given themselves over to sensuality so as to indulge in every kind of impurity, with a continual lust for more." These verses also point to ways we can avoid being caught in sexual addiction. One way is to make a choice of the will not to make the ways of the world our ways. Another point of advice is that if we want to avoid sexual impurity we should pursue a godly life and be sensitive to those things that please and offend our Lord.

God also has strong feelings about those people who feed on the weakness of human nature and appeal to people's lustful desires for their own gain: "With eyes full of adultery, they never stop sinning; they seduce the unstable; they are experts in greed—an accursed brood!...These men are springs without water and mists driven by a storm. Blackest darkness is reserved for them. For they mouth empty, boastful words and, by

Exposure to pornography affects the sexual attitudes of all those exposed—men and women alike.

appealing to the lustful desires of sinful human nature, they entice people who are just escaping from those who live in error" (2 Pet. 2:14,17,18).

From God's point of view, the actions of such people cannot be taken lightly. Christians need to voice God's outrage. Scripture tells us, "Have nothing to do with the fruitless deeds of darkness, but rather expose them" (Eph. 5:11). In order to accomplish this goal, we must be informed about what pornography has become, and the financial and social hold that the promoters of pornography have on our society. We must also take a look at the degree to which our students have been affected by these influences. We must hold fast to the truth and purity Scripture commands and at the same time develop an intense sensitivity and compassion for those who have become the victims of pornography.

As Christians and as leaders we would love to pretend that members of our congregations and our Christian students are not being infected by the proliferation of pornography in our society. But we cannot risk such optimism. The odds are that today's church youth group will have members who are being exposed to, perhaps addicted to, sexually explicit materials. Some of your students may receive Christ, yet carry with them a past of involvement with pornography. When someone becomes a Christian, the effects of this addiction don't automatically disappear. Many times the battle intensifies. You may also have students who are Christians, yet are weak in withstanding the influences of the world and controlling their sexual desires. They also are in battle and need your compassion and sensitivity. Or you may have students who have been sexually victimized by family members or peers. More often than not, they are victims of someone's use of pornography.

These students in your midst are in secret torment. Those using pornography hate their sin and yet probably feel unable to control their lust for it. Possibly they have digressed to acting out what they have seen. These people need to be challenged with the commands of Scripture, but this challenge must come with a large dose of hope for freedom from bondage. Self-righteous condemnation will do nothing to achieve the Lord's passion to bind up the brokenhearted and set the captives free (Isa. 61:1,2).

Those sexually addicted usually suffer from low self-esteem and a deep emotional pain that drives them into a world of fantasy in order to escape a painful reality.

The repeated use of pornography can be interpreted as a symptom of heart-felt emotional and spiritual need.

Their shame necessitates a double life and self-imposed secrecy to protect their fragile sense of self.

Shame is fuel for the fire of sexual addiction, so care must be taken to guard their human dignity while dealing with these deeply sensitive issues. It is important not to publicly expose them in any way, yet minister to their needs. It is best to consult a professional Christian counselor if this sort of problem is confided to you.

We must be careful to separate God's abhorrence for the debauchery of pornography from His love for those who have been corrupted by it (some through no choice of their own). Failure to do this can result in reinforcing the mistaken belief that God utterly detests those who've been the victims of sexual abuse.

Our Personal Response

At its core, this issue deals with how we relate to one another as whole persons, created by God as male and female for the purpose of godly union in marriage to become one flesh. One must see this issue through two sets of glasses and help both sexes better understand how God made them and how He intends them to relate to each other.

We must also keep in mind that our understanding of God's design for sex and relationships can become tarnished. Everyone is susceptible to negative elements in society, including the lure of pornography. Because of this, our first response to pornography must be personal. We need to consciously agree with God regarding sexual attitudes and how we will guard the purity of our sexuality. For some this will be a long process of renewing their minds (see Rom. 12:1,2; Eph. 4:22-24). For others it will be a commitment to guard their hearts and minds from elements like pornography that work against God's purposes (see Prov. 4:20-27).

Political and civic action against pornography is certainly appropriate, but it cannot be presented as all there is to do. For each person there will be occasions where he or she can influence peers as the issue arises in everyday life. You and your students need to have a clear understanding of the beauty and sanctity of godly sexuality in order to contrast this with the cheap substitute the world has to offer. Your students need to be warned that God does not call us to immerse themselves in the ways of the world in order to turn around those who are trapped by them. Psalm 1:1,2 tells us to focus our attention on the law of the Lord and not to "stand in the way of sinners." This is especially vital when dealing with something as powerful as our God-given sexuality and the corruptible nature of our flesh.

Notes

1. Richard E. McLawhorn, *Report of the Attorney General's Commission on Pornography* (Cincinnati: National Coalition Against Pornography, Inc., July 1986).
2. As reported in the *California Care Coalition Fact Sheet* (1990).
3. Miller vs. California, United States Supreme Court decision, 1973.
4. Dr. Jerry R. Kirk, *Hard Core: Already Illegal, the Case Against Hard-core Pornography in America* (Pomona, CA: Focus on the Family Publishing, 1989).
5. A 1985 study sponsored by the Canadian government. As reported to the United States Attorney General's Commission on Pornography (July 1986).
6. Dean Kaplan, *National Coalition Against Pornography* (1989).
7. Daryl F. Gates, Los Angeles Police Chief. Testimony to the United States Attorney General's Commission on Pornography (July 1986).
8. United States Department of Justice (1988).
9. This information was shared by Dr. Victor Cline in a seminar titled "The Impact of the Media on the Family" conducted at the November 10, 1990 conference of the National Coalition Against Pornography (NCAP) in Pittsburgh, Pennsylvania.
10. Dols Zillman and J. Bryant, "Pornography: Sexual Callousness and the Trivialization of Rape," *Journal of Communication* (1984), pp. 10-21. As reported in the *California Care Coalition Fact Sheet* (1989).
11. Dr. Jerry R. Kirk, *The Power of the Picture: How Pornography Harms* (Pomona, CA: Focus on the Family Publishing, 1989), p. 5.
12. This information was gathered from personal conversations with women who had become addicted to pornography and were seeking in-patient treatment to help them find freedom.
13. Dr. Jerry R. Kirk, *Mind Polluters* (Nashville: Thomas Nelson Publishers, 1985).

TEACHING PLAN

APPROACH (5-8 minutes)

Materials needed: An inexpensive wind-up alarm clock, a board with two nails partially nailed into it.

When students have gathered, present the following object lesson. Say, **I have accepted a challenge to hammer these two nails in within five minutes.** Set the alarm on the clock to ring in five minutes. Ask a student to keep an eye on the clock and let you know when your time is almost up. Then look frantically around for something to use to pound in the nails. After a moment, grab the alarm clock and begin using it to pound the nails. Ignore for the moment comments and warnings from the students. Then say something like, **Tell me when my time's up. What? Am I doing something wrong? I want to finish in time.** By now the clock will be damaged beyond use. Allow a moment for students to comment on your actions. Then ask, **Can this clock do what it was designed for? Why not?**

Then say, **Today we are going to look at how our attitudes toward sexual intimacy can be affected by the damaging influence of pornography. Like the clock was damaged when it was used inappropriately, our understanding of sexual intimacy can be damaged when ungodly images, such as those portrayed in pornography, color our thinking. How we use our sexuality now will affect our future sexuality and our relationships with others.**

ALTERNATE APPROACH (8-10 minutes)

Use this Alternate Approach instead of the Approach above if you feel your students need help grasping the depth and seriousness of the issue of pornography. Since pornography is a sensitive issue with any group, especially adolescents, it is important that the right tone for the session be set at the beginning. Evaluate the needs of your group in focusing on this topic and choose the Approach activity that best meets those needs.

Materials needed: A video- or audiotape of Dr. James Dobson's interview with serial killer Ted Bundy, audio- or videotape player and monitor. (This interview can be obtained from Focus on the Family, Pomona, CA 91799, 1-800-A-FAMILY for a small donation. You may also want to check your or other local church libraries for this resource.)

Preparation: Preview the tape before class and choose a five minute segment of the tape that you feel conveys the seriousness of the influence of pornography in the life of Ted Bundy.

Play the selected segment of the tape. Allow a moment for students to share any comments and then say, **Today we are going to look at how our attitudes toward sexual intimacy can be affected by the damaging influence of pornography. How we express our sexuality now will affect our future sexuality and our relationships with others.**

BIBLE EXPLORATION (30-40 minutes)

Materials needed: Bibles, a copy for each student of "The Downward Spiral" student worksheet, a copy for each group of three to five students of the "Who Gets Hurt?"

> We must be careful to separate God's abhorrence for the debauchery of pornography from His love for those who have been corrupted by it.

student worksheet, the "Case Study" resource page, chalkboard and chalk or newsprint and felt pen, pencils.

Step 1 (5-8 minutes)

Take a few minutes to share some statistics and general information about the influence and effects of pornography upon our society (use information from the "Defining Pornography" and "The Facts About Pornography" sections of the Teacher's Bible Study and any other resources available to you). Be sure to include the following points in your presentation:

- Pornography is the representation of sexually explicit behavior intended to arouse sexual excitement.
- Less than 10 percent of the pornographic materials available depict normal heterosexual activities between one man and one woman.
- The primary consumers of pornography are adolescent males between the ages of 12 and 17.
- Even though there are laws restricting the generation, use and availability of soft porn and hard-core pornography (including an age limitation), these laws are rarely enforced.
- Organized crime is the primary benefactor of the sale of pornographic material.
- Pornography is used by child molesters to break down their victims natural resistance. Children and women are the predominant victims of pornography—especially when those consuming pornography act out what they see.
- Pornography can have an addictive effect on its consumers and can lead to acting out sexual crimes.
- Repeated exposure to pornography results in a view of human sexuality which is degraded, harmful and increasingly dehumanized.

Step 2 (7-10 minutes)

Say, **Let's look at how the initial step of exposure to pornography leads to other harmful effects in our lives. This process is described clearly in Scripture and is supported by clinical evidence.** Distribute pencils and copies of "The Downward Spiral" student worksheet. Direct your students to individually match each effect of exposure to pornography with the Bible reference(s) describing that effect in a person's life (step 1=Jas. 1:14; step 2=2 Pet. 2:19; step 3=Eph. 4:19; step 4=Jas. 1:15).

After a few moments, discuss how repeated exposure to pornography can create a downward spiral in a person's life. Use the following questions and verses in your discussion.

- What are some ways a person can break the cycle of

pornography's effects before it reaches the point of addiction? (See Phil. 4:8; 2 Tim. 2:22; Jas. 1:21; 5:16.)

- How can we respond to a person who uses pornography? (Discuss the relationship between Eph. 4:2,32 and 5:11.)
- According to Ephesians 4:19, people who have "lost all sensitivity" and "have given themselves over to sensuality" are out of control and lose sight of clear lines between right and wrong. If we see a Christian friend in this state, what can we do to help that friend? (See Gal. 6:1; Jas. 5:19,20; 1 Pet. 4:8.)
- Mark 7:21 says that sexual sin comes from evil thoughts in our hearts. What can a person do to purify his or her heart of such thoughts and find healing from the effects of pornography? (See 1 John 1:9.)

Step 3 (8-10 minutes)

Say, **Evidence shows that exposure to pornography can affect who you are—your attitudes toward yourself, your relationship with God and your relationships with others. Proverbs 4:23 tells us that to protect the quality of our lives we need to guard our hearts.** Read aloud, or ask a volunteer to read aloud, Proverbs 4:23. As a group, list on the chalkboard or newsprint situations through which pornography can enter a person's heart and mind. Ask students to suggest ways to guard their hearts in each of the situations listed. You may want to discuss several of the situations listed below.

- You are spending the weekend with a friend. His or her parents are out of town and you accidentally run across some pornographic magazines at your friend's house. How do you guard your heart?
- You're watching TV alone. While flipping the channels you run across a sexually explicit scene on a cable channel. How do you guard your heart?
- You're (a guy) at a party and some of the guys go off into another room. You join them only to find that they are heartily watching a pornographic video. Three of them attend your church youth group. How do you guard your heart?
- You're hanging out at the local convenience store with two friends. One of them picks up a "soft-porn" magazine and calls you over to look. How do you guard your heart?
- You're a girl who's infatuated (i.e., "madly in love with") a very popular guy. You're the envy of all your friends because you've dated him a few times. He asks you to come over and watch a movie at his house. You have agreed. When he picks you up you see the videos he has chosen sitting on the car seat.

The titles of the videos are sexually suggestive. How do you guard your heart?

Step 4 (10-12 minutes)

Introduce this step by saying, **Pornography affects more that just the person viewing it. One person's use of pornography can extend harm to countless other people. Let's look at who gets hurt by pornography.** Move your students into groups of three to five. All members of an individual group should be of the same gender.

Say, **I am going to read a story that represents what can realistically happen when a person becomes entrapped by the lure of pornography.** Read aloud the story on the "Case Study" resource page. Then distribute one copy of the "Who Gets Hurt?" student worksheet to each group. Say, **In your groups work together to write your answers to each of the questions on the worksheet. Do not write your names on the sheet. Simply indicate the gender of the members of your group.**

Allow five to eight minutes for students to work. If discussions among the group members are going well, you may want to allow as much time as possible for this activity.

When time for the groups to work is up, collect the worksheets. Anonymously share some of the comments the groups wrote at the bottom of their sheets concerning how pornography affects the attitudes of those who use it, and who gets hurt by the use of pornography.

Make a comparison between what the girls wrote and what the guys wrote. Ask students to share their thoughts on the different ways guys and girls understand the affects of pornography. As necessary, share information on the difference between how men and women respond to sexual stimulants (see the end of "The Facts About Pornography" section of the Teacher's Bible Study for more information on this subject).

Move to the Conclusion by saying, **We have seen that pornography does have a negative effect on relationships, society and a person's spiritual condition. Let's look at how we can personally respond to pornography and protect ourselves from its harmful effects.**

CONCLUSION (8-10 minutes)

Materials needed: Scratch paper and pencils. Optional—a recording of Leslie Phillips' song "Your Kindness" from the album titled *Black and White in a Grey World* (available from Myrrh Records) and a means by which you can play the recording for the class (cassette player, etc.).

Distribute the scratch paper and pencils. Then tell the students that they will individually write on their papers their responses to several questions you will read out loud. Read aloud the following questions, allowing time between each question for students to write their responses.

- In what one way are you most vulnerable to exposure to or influence from pornography?
- What activities in your life negatively influence your attitudes to members of the opposite sex or your own sexuality? (You may want the students to evaluate the point at which activities such as reading romance novels, watching soap operas or MTV, reading magazines or their choice of movies and friends blur their understanding of how God views human sexuality.)
- After considering the areas where you are most vulnerable, where would you draw the line limiting your involvement in activities that weaken your understanding of God's view of sexuality? (Suggest that students evaluate an activity in terms of whether or not they would feel comfortable participating in that activity if they were aware of Jesus' presence with them at the time. Also mention that most people underestimate their level of resistance to negative influences.)
- What is one step you can take to strengthen your understanding of God's perspective of human sexuality?
- What is one thing you can do personally to combat the influence of pornography in your world?

After students have considered these questions say, **All of us have areas of our lives that don't measure up to God's standards, and this can be depressing. But we must remember that our sexuality is a precious gift from God. Even if it has been damaged the Lord can renew our minds and restore our broken lives. He makes forgiveness available to any person that comes to Him and asks for it. And He can provide us with Christian friends we can share our needs with and who can support us as we try to make changes in how we live.** Invite any students who wish to talk further with you to remain after the session is over.

Close with audible prayer asking God to strengthen each student to withstand the negative effects pornography can have on their sexuality. Optional—have a time of silent prayer as you play Leslie Phillips' recording of "Your Kindness." Be available after class to meet with any students who express a desire to talk with you.

Resources to Consider

To point the way toward restoration for those who are already tied into using pornography, you may want to suggest the 12-step program outlined in the workbook, *Twelve Steps—A Spiritual Journey,* published by Recovery Publications, 1201 Knoxville Street, San Diego, CA 92110. In this book the 12 steps of recovery from addiction supported by Alcoholics Anonymous are listed along with corresponding Scriptures.

You may also want to make available to your students the following names of organizations and resources that can help them fight against the influence of pornography.

Information on pornography and the fight against pornography:

- Focus on the Family, Attention: Correspondence, Pomona, CA 91799, 1-800-A-FAMILY (for placing orders);
- National Coalition Against Pornography, 800 Compton Road #9224, Cincinnati, OH 45231;
- *Raising PG Kids in an X-Rated Society* by Tipper Gore (Nashville: Abingdon Press, 1987).

Information regarding helping someone who is a victim of pornography and/or sexual abuse:

- California Care Coalition, P.O. Box 94566, Pasadena, CA 91109 (818)564-1076 (or your local child protective services agency). Note: It is a United States federal law that suspected or reported sexual abuse of a minor be reported to the local child protective services. For the safety of the victim, you are legally responsible to report this to the proper authorities. Under *no* circumstances is it advised that you try to confront the abuser directly. If a situation such as this should come to your attention, also notify your senior pastor.

Information on helping someone who is struggling with a sexual addiction:

- New Life Treatment Center, (800)332-TEEN (for adolescents) or (800)227-LIFE (for adults), Western Medical Center, Anaheim, CA.

STUDENT WORKSHEETS AND RESOURCE PAGES

The following pages contain the Student Worksheets and Resource Pages for this course.

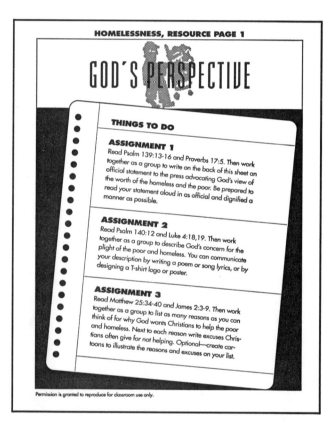

For further instructions, please read pages 8,9.

A HELPFUL NOTE:

It is NOT necessary for you to make copies of every Student Worksheet or Resource Page for each session!
- Worksheets may be made into overhead projector transparencies for the class to read. (Warning: Be sure to use the kind of transparency designed for use in copiers. If the copier jams, ordinary acetate plastic melts inside a hot copier!)

- The editors of this course recognize that too much of a good thing—even handouts—can be too much. Seek variety in your teaching times. Spice up your classes with a guest speaker, or show a good Christian film for discussion. Even a trip to the donut shop can give you an opportunity to minister to your students!

IMAGES OF HEAVEN AND HELL

The Bible provides us with glimpses of what heaven and hell are like. After reading the following Scriptures, write what each passage says about heaven and/or hell.

Scripture   **Characteristic(s) of Heaven and/or Hell**

Luke 16:23-26

Matthew 25:41

2 Thessalonians 1:8-10

Revelation 7:15-17

Revelation 21:3,4

Revelation 21:23-27

1 Peter 1:3,4

John 14:2,3

Revelation 14:9-13

ABRAHAMIC COVENANT

Complete the sentences by looking up the verses. Read the completed description of the promises God made to Abraham, then answer the questions at the bottom of the page.

The _____ (Genesis 12:1) said to _____, (v. 1)....

"Go _____ (v. 1).

I will _____ and I will _____ (v. 2);

I will _____ (v. 2), and you will _____ (v. 2).

I will _____ (v. 3), and whoever _____ (v. 3)

you I will _____ (v. 3); and _____ (v. 3)

on earth will be _____ (v. 3) through _____ (v. 3)."

"I will _____ (Genesis 17:7) as an _____ (v. 7)

covenant between _____ (v. 7) and _____ (v. 7)

after you for the _____ (v. 7) to come, to be _____ (v. 7)

and the _____ (v. 7) of _____ (v. 7)

after you....You are to undergo _____ (v. 11), and it will be the

sign of the _____ (v. 11) between me and you....My covenant in your

_____ (v. 13) is to be an _____ (v. 13) covenant."

What does God promise in this covenant?

What conditions did God require of Abraham's descendants in order for this covenant to be in effect?

Read Hebrews 6:13-18. How do these verses describe God's covenant with Abraham?

DAVIDIC COVENANT

Complete the sentences by looking up the verses. Read the completed description of the promises God made to David, then answer the questions at the bottom of the page.

"The Lord himself will establish a _____ (2 Samuel 7:11) for you:... I will raise up your _____ (v. 12) to succeed you....I will establish the _____ (v. 13) of his _____ (v. 13)....When he does wrong, I will _____ (v. 14) him with the _____ (v. 14) of _____ (v. 14)....But my _____ (v. 15) will _____ (v. 15) be taken away from him....Your _____ (v. 16) and your _____ (v. 16) will endure _____ (v. 16) before me; your _____ (v. 16) will be established _____ (v. 16)."

"I have found _____ (Psalm 89:20) my servant; with my sacred oil I have _____ (v. 20) him....I will _____ (v. 28) my _____ (v. 28) to him _____ (v. 28), and my _____ (v. 28) with him will _____ (v. 28). I will establish his _____ (v. 29), his throne as long as the _____ (v. 29). If his sons forsake my law and do not follow my statutes, if they violate my decrees and _____ (v. 31), I will _____ (v. 32) their sin with the _____ (v. 32), their _____ (v. 32) with _____ (v. 32); but I will not take my _____ (v. 33) from him....I will not _____ (v. 34) my covenant or _____ (v. 34) what my lips have uttered. Once for all, I have _____ (v. 35) by my _____ (v. 35)...that his line will continue _____ (v. 36) and his throne endure before me like the _____ (v. 36); it will be established _____ (v. 37) like the _____ (v. 37), the _____ (v. 37) in the _____ (v. 37)."

What did God promise David and his descendants?

What conditions did God place on David's descendants in order for God to keep this covenant?

What signs did God say would designate how long the kingdom would belong to David's descendants?

What do these signs tell you about how long these promises will belong to David's descendants?

PALESTINIAN COVENANT

Complete the sentences by looking up the verses. Read the completed description of the promises God made to the nation of Israel (Abraham's descendants), then answer the questions at the bottom of the page.

"The Lord appeared to Abram and said, 'To _____ (Genesis 12:7) I will _____ (v. 7).... _____ (Genesis 13:15) that you see I will _____ (v. 15) to _____ (v. 15) and your _____ (v. 15). I will make your _____ (v. 16) like the _____ (v. 16) of the earth, so that if anyone could count the dust, then your _____ (v. 16) could be _____ (v. 16).'"

"On that day the _____ (Genesis 15:18) made a _____ (v. 18) with _____ (v. 18) and said, 'To _____ (v. 18) I _____ (v. 18) this _____ (v. 18), from the river of _____ (v. 18) to the great river, _____ (v. 18)—the _____ (v. 19) of the Kenites, Kenizzites, Kadmonites, Hittites, Perizzites, Rephaites, Amorites, Canaanites, Girgashites and Jebusites.'"

"I will take the _____ (Ezekiel 37:21) out of the _____ (v. 21) where they have gone. I will _____ (v. 21) them from _____ (v. 21) and bring them _____ (v. 21) into their _____ (v. 21)....I will _____ (v. 23) them from all their _____ (v. 23), and I will _____ (v. 23) them. They will be _____ (v. 23), and I will be _____ (v. 23)."

What promises did God make to the nation of Israel.

Read Genesis 17:7,8. How do these verses describe God's promise of a land for the Jewish people?

What conditions must the people of Israel fulfill in order for the covenant to be valid?

Complete the sentences by looking up the verses. Read the completed description of the promises God made to the nation of Israel, then answer the questions at the bottom of the page.

"'The time is coming,' declares the Lord, 'when I will make a _____ _____ (Jeremiah 31:31) with the house of _____ (v 31) and with the house of _____ (v. 31)....I will put my _____ (v. 33) in their _____ (v. 33) and write it on their _____ (v. 33). I will be _____ (v. 33) God, and they will be _____ (v. 33)....I will _____ (v. 34) their _____ (v. 34) and will remember their _____ (v. 34) no more.'...He who appoints the _____ (v. 35) to shine by _____ (v. 35), who decrees the _____ (v. 35) and _____ (v. 35) to shine by _____ (v. 35), who stirs up the sea so that it's _____ (v. 35) roar....This is what the Lord says: 'Only if the _____ (v. 37) above can be _____ (v. 37) and the _____ (v. 37) of the _____ (v. 37) below be searched out will I _____ (v. 37) all the _____ (v. 37) of Israel because of all they have _____ (v. 37),' declares the _____" (v. 37).

What does God promise in this covenant?

How long will it be before the people of Israel cease to be a nation before the Lord?

What would have to happen for God to reject Israel because of her sins? Is it possible for these things to happen?

Make copies of this page, then cut the copies apart along the lines. Assemble each of the four sections of the page into separate groups to distribute to the students.

NAZI POLICE

- You believe that the Jews are the cause of all the world's problems and that God has made you superior to them.
- You have the legal right and power to enforce all rules established against the Jews: confining them to the ghetto, confiscating all food and Bibles.
- You have the right to harass, command, bully, imprison or mark for extermination any Jew you feel is being disobedient or disrespectful.
- It is your duty to move all Jews to the ghetto and keep them from interacting with non-Jews. You must also make sure that everyone is wearing his or her identifying symbol.
- You may use ordinary citizens or Christians to help you in all of the above tasks (as informants, etc.). Any ordinary citizens or Christians who break the rules must be put in prison. Those who help the Jews may be marked for extermination.

JEWS

- You will be punished if you leave the ghetto area.
- The government has decreed that all food, Bibles and other necessities should be confiscated from you.
- You are responsible for responding to the Nazi police with obedience and respect.
- You can be sent to prison or marked for extermination by the police. If you are sent to prison, go to the prison area. If you are marked for extermination, go to the graveyard. Ordinary citizens and Christians may help you or they may be informants against you for the police.

ORDINARY CITIZEN

- You are an ordinary citizen who does not have any moral convictions. You are simply concerned about taking care of your own best interests. You may choose to ignore what is happening to the Jews, but you are responsible to obey the police.
- You may choose to help the police by informing on anyone who is a Jew, attempts to help the Jews or breaks the rules.
- You may help the Jews if you choose to do so, but you risk being sent to prison or marked for extermination (sent to the graveyard).
- You may bully the Jews in order to gain favor with the police, or as a cover for aid you are giving to the Jews.

CHRISTIAN

- You are responsible to obey the Lord concerning the circumstances around you.
- You can be imprisoned or marked for extermination (sent to the graveyard) if you help the Jews.
- You may help the Jews by praying for them, providing them with food, giving words of support and encouragement, concealing their identities.
- You may choose to be silent and protect yourself from being sent to prison.
- Your obedience and respect are expected from the police.

CREATION: GOD'S GIFT, OUR RESPONSIBILITY

God and Creation

1. What does the natural beauty of creation give to God? (See Psalm 19:1.)

   With what attitude does the psalmist respond, when he reflects upon the magnificence of God's creation? (See Psalm 136:1-9.)

2. How does God view what He created? (See Genesis 1:31.)

   As expressed in Luke 12:6,7, describe God's care for the smallest as well as the most valuable of His creatures.

3. What are some conservation and waste disposal techniques God established for His people? (See Leviticus 25:3-5,8-12; Deuteronomy 23:12,13.)

4. What did Jesus say about wastefulness? (See John 6:12.)

People and Creation

1. What responsibility was Adam given for the Garden of Eden and consequently for all of creation? (See Genesis 2:15.)

2. What role did God give humankind in relationship to creation? (See Genesis 1:26,28; Psalm 8:3-8.)

3. Describe what happened to the relationship between people and God's creation when Adam and Eve rebelled against Him. (See Genesis 3:17-19.)

   How do you think this change has affected people's ability to subdue, or take control of, the earth? To care for it?

4. If we do not honor and obey God and respect and cherish His creation, how might our relationship with the environment be affected? (See Deuteronomy 28:15,38-42.)

   If we honor and obey God and respect and cherish His creation, how might our relationship with the environment be affected? (See Deuteronomy 28:1-8; 2 Chronicles 7:13,14.)

WHAT WE CAN DO

1. Drive less
    A. Use public transportation
    B. Car pool
    C. Take only essential trips
    D. Do as many errands as possible by mail
    E. Ride a bicycle or walk to get where you need to go
2. Use less electricity and natural gas
    A. Lower your thermostat in the winter
    B. Improve the insulation in your home
    C. Install an energy efficient furnace
    D. Use less hot water
    E. In summer, set your thermostat higher
    F. Install energy efficient appliances (check the Energy Efficiency Rating [EER] on the labels)
    G. Shade your house naturally in hot climates
    H. Turn lights on conservatively; use fluorescent bulbs and lower wattage bulbs
    I. Use appliances less
3. Use solar energy
    A. Dry clothes in the sun
    B. Install solar panels to heat your house and water
4. Plant trees and other vegetation; preserve existing vegetation—this will improve the air quality and contribute to slowing the rate of global warming
5. Use non-toxic pest control
    A. Use diatomaceous earth to get rid of slugs (an organic substance available from your local nursery)
    B. Use insects like ladybugs to get rid of other insect pests
    C. Use biological control of insect populations
    D. Do old fashioned weeding instead of using herbicides (weed killers)
6. Use substitutes for lead shot, leaded gasoline, aerosol sprays and refrigerants
7. Recycle paper, metals (aluminum and steel cans), glass and plastics
8. Try to convince other people to conserve energy and recycle
9. Get involved in groups that are implementing workable solutions to preserve creation
10. To your representatives in government, write letters that support saving God's creation
11. Pray for God's help to save His creation

LET'S DEBATE

- ✂

"Should we try to save endangered species?"

PRO Endangered species must be saved, even if it requires that people experience inconvenience or discomfort. Over half of all known species are predicted to go extinct in this century. In 1970 the number of species on the official United States endangered and threatened species list was 92. In 1989 there were 539.[*] The account of Noah (see Genesis 7:1-5) indicates that God is concerned about the survival of each species. As stewards of God's creation, we have done an embarrassing job of preserving the earth. We have abused our privileges as rulers of the earth in order to indulge our own selfish desires. We must not delay in fulfilling our responsibilities toward creation. Protecting endangered species is one area in which we can be good stewards, following God's desire for the earth He has given us.

[*]From *National Wildlife* (February/March 1990).

- ✂

"Should we try to save endangered species?"

CON Although preserving and caring for God's creation is an important role given to humankind, this responsibility must be balanced with God's command to people to subdue, or take control of, the earth and rule over it (see Genesis 1:28). For example, the reduction of timber harvests by nearly half to save the spotted owl in the forests of Washington, Oregon and Northern California could cost people in the region 28,000 jobs over a span of 10 years. A federal study predicts that this loss of jobs will result in destroying timber towns and increasing rates of violence, divorce and suicide.[**] Preserving the species at the expense of basic human needs is not according to God's purpose for people. Matthew 10:29-31 says, "Are not two sparrows sold for a penny? Yet not one of them will fall to the ground apart from the will of your Father. And even the very hairs of your head are all numbered. So don't be afraid; you are worth more than many sparrows." We hope that ways can be found to preserve the species, but not at the cost of the needs of God's more valuable creation: people.

[**]From *The Spokesman-Review Spokane Chronicle* (June 24, 1990).

HOW TO CONTROL ANGER

1. Read Galatians 5:20. Among other things, this verse lists "fits of rage" as an act of the sinful nature. How is a fit of rage different from just feeling anger?

   Galatians 5:22,23 lists the "fruit of the Spirit." Which fruit can help you avoid "fits of rage?" _____ control (fill in the blank).

2. Some very practical suggestions for controlling anger are given in Proverbs 14:29, 15:18 and 19:11. List below ways these verses say you can respond to an angry situation.

   James 1:19,20 also gives a good suggestion for controlling anger. It says we should be _____ to _____. What can result if you apply this suggestion to your life?

3. Forgiveness is an essential element in dealing with anger. Ephesians 4:31,32 says we can deal with anger by getting get rid of some things and replacing them with others.

   We are to get rid of: We are to be:

4. Usually when someone treats us badly we want to get even. But Jesus said we should love our enemies. Read Matthew 5:43,44. Another way to deal with anger is to _____ the people who mistreat us.

Four Things We Can Do to Control Anger

1. Pray for self-_____.

2. Be _____ to anger.

3. F_____ the person who wronged you.

4. L_____ your enemies.

MY PERSONAL MEDIA USE PLAN

1. How much time each week will I spend with each of the following forms of media?

Forms of Media	Hours Per Week
Television	_____
Radio	_____
Movies	_____
Records/tapes/cd's	_____
Magazines	_____
Books	_____
Total media time per week:	_____

2. How will I select which programs (radio, television), tapes, movies or books I will spend time with? (Check as many as apply.)
   - _____ Plop down and watch or listen to whatever is on.
   - _____ Watch and listen to whatever my friends or family choose.
   - _____ Use a television guide/movie reviews to select programs.
   - _____ Choose programs that are not too violent or sexy.
   - _____ Change the channel/turn pages when the content is inappropriate.
   - _____ Choose programs that will help me grow spiritually.

3. How will I make use of Christian media? In the next two weeks I will:
   - _____ Check out a Christian book from the church library.
   - _____ Listen to a Christian radio station.
   - _____ Watch a Christian television station.
   - _____ Watch a Christian video.
   - _____ Visit a Christian bookstore.
   - _____ Other _____.

4. How will I evaluate what I see in the media in terms of what the Bible teaches (right and wrong, good and bad). In the next month I will:
   - _____ Go to a movie with Christian friends and discuss how the values the movie portrayed agree/disagree with Christian values.
   - _____ Watch and discuss with friends or family the values presented in a popular television program.
   - _____ Discuss with a friend or family member the values depicted in the advertisements and articles in a popular magazine.
   - _____ Listen to several popular songs. Discuss with family or friends the values presented in each song.
   - _____ Other _____.

As you listen to the song, write your responses to the following questions.

1. How would God want a Christian to respond to the struggle of the poor and homeless?

2. How does this song say God feels about the injustices the poor and homeless experience?

3. What are some ways a Christian can respond to the needs of the poor and homeless?

GOD'S PERSPECTIVE

THINGS TO DO

ASSIGNMENT 1

Read Psalm 139:13-16 and Proverbs 17:5. Then work together as a group to write on the back of this sheet an official statement to the press advocating God's view of the worth of the homeless and the poor. Be prepared to read your statement aloud in as official and dignified a manner as possible.

ASSIGNMENT 2

Read Psalm 140:12 and Luke 4:18,19. Then work together as a group to describe God's concern for the plight of the poor and homeless. You can communicate your description by writing a poem or song lyrics, or by designing a T-shirt logo or poster.

ASSIGNMENT 3

Read Matthew 25:34-40 and James 2:3-9. Then work together as a group to list as many reasons as you can think of for why God wants Christians to help the poor and homeless. Next to each reason write excuses Christians often give for not helping. Optional—create cartoons to illustrate the reasons and excuses on your list.

PUT-DOWNS VS. BUILD-UPS

Bible Build-ups

Have someone in your group read each Bible verse out loud. Work together to complete the chart.

	What do these verses say about the words we speak?
Proverbs 16:24	
Ephesians 4:29	
1 Thessalonians 5:11	
James 3:7-10	

Sound Familiar?

Carefully examine the case studies below. Think of detailed and practical ways to apply any or all of the above Scriptures to each situation. Think of two or three responses for each situation.

1. Sam is taking the bus home after school. His math teacher hops aboard and sits next to him. Math is Sam's worst subject. What are some things the teacher can say to Sam to fulfill the Bible verses above about building others up. What are some ways Sam can build up his teacher? (Hint: If you were a teacher, what would you want to hear from your students?)

2. Sally shoots from the lip—she insults and yells at her good friend Jennifer. Now Sally is sorry. "Why can't I keep my big mouth shut?" she moans to herself. She really didn't mean what she said. Jennifer storms off. If you were Brenda, a good friend of both girls, how can you encourage and build both friends up? (Hint: Is there a special place you three can meet together?)

3. You and your friends enjoy your youth group very much. You're excited about Jesus and want to live for Him. One night, three new kids show up. They are noisy and disturb the Bible study. Afterward, they smoke outdoors and talk crudely. What can you and your friends say to them? (Hint: Are there other youth group activities you can invite them to?)

4. Create your own situation! Work together in your group to come up with a typical family conflict—parents versus kid or older child versus younger child. Figure out some ways to change the conflict into a victory by employing the wisdom from the Bible.

CONSEQUENCES OF COMPROMISE

Look up the verses next to the names. Match the names with the corresponding compromises of integrity and the resulting consequences.

PERSON	COMPROMISE	CONSEQUENCES
Achan: Joshua 7:1,20-26	Collected payment from a man for God's miraculous healing.	Child died.
Ananias and Sapphira: Acts 5:1-11	Rebelled against Moses' God-given authority.	Committed suicide.
Gehazi: 2 Kings 5:14-27	Committed adultery and murder.	Ground opened and swallowed him, his family and his men.
Adam and Eve: Genesis 2:16,17; 3:6,22-24; Romans 5:12-14	Betrayed Jesus Christ for 30 pieces of silver.	He and his family were stoned to death.
Ten spies and the Israelites: Numbers 13:1,2, 26—14:4,34	Disobeyed God in spite of His warning of death.	Contracted leprosy.
David: 2 Samuel 11:2-5, 14,15; 12:11-18	Doubted God's ability to give Israel their promised land.	Struck dead.
Korah: Numbers 16:1-3, 28-34	Stole gold, silver and a beautiful robe.	Wandered in the wilderness for 40 years.
Judas: Matthew 27:3-5	Lied to God.	Brought sin and death to the whole human race.

KEEPING INTEGRITY INTACT

The people described below maintained their integrity in spite of difficult circumstances. Read the verses to find the name of each person. Then write one positive thing that happened because the person maintained his integrity.

1. He submitted Himself to unimaginable physical torment rather than disobey what God had planned for Him (read John 3:16,17 and Philippians 2:8).
   Name:
   A positive result:

2. This person willingly faced the jeering of his neighbors as he obeyed God's instructions to prepare for a flood—even though the possibility of rain seemed impossible (read Genesis 6:11-22 and 2 Peter 2:5).
   Name:
   A positive result:

3. He put his life on the line by challenging 850 prophets of false gods (read 1 Kings 18:18,19,36-39).
   Name:
   A positive result:

4. They suffered imprisonment because they refused to stop telling others about Jesus—even though the governing officials commanded them to stop (read Acts 4:18-22).
   Names:
   A positive result:

5. They were thrown into a fiery furnace because they refused to worship an idol (read Daniel 3:16-18).
   Names:
   A positive result:

6. In spite of the efforts of a woman to seduce him and the feelings of loneliness this slave must have had, he refused to disobey God—even though he was falsely accused of rape and thrown in jail (read Genesis 39:7-23).
   Name:
   A positive result:

GOD'S DESIGN FOR FAMILIES

Divide the following verses among the members of your group. Read your assigned verses then, as a group, answer the questions according to what these verses say children and parents can do to function as a healthy family.

Deuteronomy 5:16
Deuteronomy 6:6,7
Deuteronomy 27:16
Proverbs 23:22
Ephesians 4:29

Ephesians 4:30-32
Ephesians 6:1-4
Colossians 3:13
Colossians 3:20,21
1 Thessalonians 2:11,12

What attitudes should family members have?

What actions can parents take to live according to God's design?

What actions can children take to live according to God's design?

FACING THE PROBLEM

Choose and complete one of the following assignments.

ASSIGNMENT #1

If you are the son or daughter of a parent who abuses substances, you should remember a few things about your situation:

1. It is not your fault. Your parent is responsible for his or her own actions.
2. It is not uncommon. Other kids your age are struggling too.
3. It is not easy to change. You can't control your parent's life.
4. You can make choices about how you will react to your home situation and the impact it is having on you—emotionally, spiritually and relationally.

Consider the following questions.

In what ways can you rely on God to help you deal with your parent(s)?

What can you do to show obedience and respect to your parent—even though he or she may not seem to deserve it?

Who can you turn to for support and encouragement? Plan to talk to a friend, counselor or contact an organization that addresses substance abuse (ask your leader for the names of people you can contact).

ASSIGNMENT #2

You may not have a parent who abuses substances, but chances are you have a friend or family member who does.

Consider what action you could take to help someone deal with a home situation where a substance abusing parent is present. Following are some suggestions. Add two or three ideas of your own to the list.

• Talk to your friend about how God can help him or her deal with the situation.
• Pray with your friend.
• Offer support and encouragement to your friend by calling or writing to him or her.
• Offer to go with your friend to a meeting with a counselor or pastor.

Circle one of the items above that describes an action you want to take to help your friend. Plan a time this week to express this help to him or her.

Use these cards if you need help or know a friend who does.

When there's trouble in your home...

Do you see even one of the following in your home?

- Drug paraphernalia, marijuana seeds or drugs
- Violent behavior by a family member
- Physical or sexual abuse of a family member
- A family member showing dramatic changes in appearance, mood or behavior
- Family members being arrested or involved in accidents because of substance abuse
- A family member getting drunk or high on drugs on a regular basis
- The presence of others who drink heavily or do drugs

Call for HELP!

1. Remove yourself immediately from any danger or harm.
2. Dial for emergency medical treatment if necessary. Many areas use 911 as an emergency number.
3. Call a pastor for support.
   The number is:
4. Call a professional for advice.
   The number is:
5. Get the support of a group of people. (Alanon, Alateen, etc.)
6. Educate yourself on substance abuse and recovery.

This information has been distributed by:

Do you need support?

- Have you been hurt or embarrassed by someone else's drinking?
- Do you lie to cover up for another person's drinking or drug use?
- Do you feel you are to blame in any way for an abuser's addiction?
- Do you feel your problems would be solved if the substance abuser in your life kicked his or her habit?
- Do you unjustly express anger toward others because you are angry at a substance abuser in your life?
- Do you feel that no one understands your problems?
- Are you afraid to upset someone because you feel you will cause the person to set off on a drinking bout or take drugs?

If you answered "yes" to any of these questions, there are people who can help you deal with the struggles in your life!

Where to find support:

- Alateen
  The number is:
- New Life Treatment Centers, Inc.
  The number is: 1-800-332-TEEN
- National Youth Crisis Hotline
  The number is: 1-800-HIT HOME
- Our pastor
  The number is:
- A professional counselor
  The number is:

This information has been distributed by:

THE DOWNWARD SPIRAL

As described by the four steps below, repeated exposure to pornography can draw a person into a downward spiral. These steps are defined by Dr. Victor Cline* and are supported by Scripture. Draw a line from each of these steps to the Bible verse(s) that describe the effect each step can have in a person's life.

Step 1: Addiction
(Being drawn back for more)

"They promise them freedom, while they themselves are slaves of depravity—for a man is a slave to whatever has mastered him." 2 Peter 2:19

Step 2: Escalation
(Needing more stimulation to get the previous level of arousal)

"But each one is tempted when, by his own evil desire, he is dragged away and enticed." James 1:14

Step 3: Desensitization
(Growing to accept things we once knew were wrong)

"Then, after desire has conceived, it gives birth to sin; and sin, when it is full-grown, gives birth to death." James 1:15

Step 4: Acting Out
(Doing some of the things described in the pornography)

"Having lost all sensitivity, they have given themselves over to sensuality so as to indulge in every kind of impurity, with a continual lust for more." Ephesians 4:19

*Based on information shared by Dr. Victor Cline at the November 10, 1990 conference of the National Coalition Against Pornography (NCAP).

WHO GETS HURT?

Do not write your names. Check one of the following to designate the gender of your group:

GUYS_____ GIRLS_____

As a group, write down specific effects the use of pornography might have on the following relationships:

• Bob's relationship with himself, that is, his self-image as a Christian man and as a sexual person.

• Bob's relationship with God.

• Bob's relationship with his fiancée.

• The girl Bob attempted to rape and her relationship with men.

• The effects on the young men in Bob's youth group (those in sexual sin and those not involved in sexual immorality).

• The effects on the young women in Bob's youth group.

• The effects on Bob's senior pastor and church leaders.

As a group, list three ways you think pornography affects the attitudes of those who use it repeatedly.

What does it destroy?

Who gets hurt?

There was a young man we will call Bob. Bob was very shy and inhibited. He found it difficult to make friends or feel like he could fit into the group of ninth graders in his class. The summer before his sophomore year Bob was befriended by an older boy named Jonathan. When they were alone, Jonathan brought out some magazines which were sexually explicit. Although Bob wasn't sure he should look at the magazines, he did not want to lose his new friend or look as though he was immature. He was also very curious. They viewed the material together and became involved in some sexually arousing activities. Bob was terribly ashamed but he was also drawn in by the excitement. This was the beginning of a fantasy life which he kept secret for many years.

Even though Bob was a Christian, he was drawn more and more into the use of pornography. He always asked God's forgiveness for using the pornographic materials, and he tried to be a good Christian. In fact, from the outside he seemed to be above average in his Christian walk. But this one area of his life was kept separate and secret from his Christian friends and activities.

Eventually Bob decided that God wanted him to become the youth pastor at the church where he had grown up. He had been dating a girl he had known since high school and they were planning to be married the following year.

Yet Bob's other life, which was controlled by the use of pornography, was out of control.

Over the years his "tastes" changed and he craved more and more explicit, even violent, sexual depictions to give him the "high" he hungered for. He would often sneak into an adult book store in a neighboring city to find what he was looking for. He seemed to be dying inside but felt that he couldn't talk to anyone. At one point he did try to explain his struggle to his senior pastor. The pastor prayed with him and gave him several passages of Scripture to read, but he didn't seem to want to believe how much of a grip this thing had on Bob. Bob didn't know who else to turn to. Who would understand?

Finally Bob's cravings were no longer satisfied with just looking. Fantasies were not enough. He began to lust after experiencing some of the sexually aggressive behavior he had seen. One night, while in a darkened parking structure, he saw a young woman walking alone. The urges inside him took control and he followed her to her car. His mind raced as fantasy swirled into reality. He forced himself into her car and with his hands on her throat prepared to act out the rape he had visualized so many times.

Suddenly, reality hit and he knew he couldn't finish what he had started. He apologized to the terrified young woman, ran back to his car and sped away—but not before she was able to get his license plate number. Bob was arrested and convicted on attempted rape. The church stripped Bob of his ministry and abandoned him. Bob was left alone to try to pick up the pieces of his life.

DESIGN-IT-YOURSELF!

The following reproducible pages contain a flyer you can use to promote this course, a Bible reading chart that you can customize to provide your students with the resources for a daily time with God and a letter to parents that will help extend your teaching into the home and express support for the parents of your students.

For further instructions, please read pages 8,9.

▬ ▬ ▬ ▬ ▬ ▬ ▬ ▬ ▬ ▬ ▬ ▬ ▬ ▬ ▬

Special note: To help you design your own materials, several books are available from Gospel Light Publications—**Magnetic Flyers, The Youth Worker's Clip Art Book, The Youth Worker's Son of Clip Art Book, I Was a Teenage Clip Art Book** and **The Bible Visual Resource Book.**

A GROUP STUDY OF NINE CRITICAL ISSUES FACING TODAY'S YOUTH

ISSUES FROM THE EDGE

PERSONAL INTEGRITY

THE ENVIRONMENT

PORNOGRAPHY

WHEN PARENTS ARE SUBSTANCE ABUSERS

LIFE AFTER DEATH

ANTI-SEMITISM

MEDIA VIOLENCE

HOMELESSNESS

PUT-DOWNS

WHAT DOES GOD HAVE TO SAY ABOUT:

• THE ENVIRONMENT • HOMELESSNESS • MEDIA VIOLENCE • PORNOGRAPHY?

Come and find out how what God thinks about these issues and more!

Who:_____

When:_____

Where:_____

BIBLE READING CHART

Scripture:

_____

Memory Verse:

_____

Reading Assignment:	
Day 1:	
Day 2:	
Day 3:	
Day 4:	
Day 5:	
Day 6:	
Day 7:	

Dear Parent,

It is exciting to see the students in our group being challenged and growing in their faith! The topics we are studying really meet them where they are. And learning what God's Word says about these issues can really make a difference in the life decisions they make.

Because parents and family are the primary influence in our students' lives, we know that your conversations with your teen on these topics can have a significant impact. To help you as you talk with your teenager, we want to provide you with Scriptures and some discussion helps that will address the topics of our Bible studies.

This week we will be discussing:

Scriptures we will be looking at:

Questions and discussion starters that will help you interact with your teenager on this topic:

Thank you for the privilege of spending time with your teen. Please let us know of ways we can support you and your family.

In Christ,

SUGGESTED RESOURCES*

for use with your basic text, the Bible.

Hot Buttons and ***Hot Buttons II*** give insights from God's Word on 24 burning issues including sex, rock music, AIDS, suicide and divorce.

"Hi, I'm Bob and I'm the Parent of a Teenager" by Tim Smith is a 7-session course designed to help parents face the unique challenges of parenting their teens.

So, What's a Christian Anyway? is a fun and simple way to explain salvation and the basics of Christianity to youth. It contains articles and games on how to use the Bible, belief, prayer, commitment and more. Order one for each of your students.

The Youth Worker's Book of Case Studies by Jim Burns presents real-life moral questions to teenagers for group discussion and learning. Scripture references and discussion questions are included.

Outrageous Object Lessons by E.G. Von Trutzschler will rivet your students' attention on the truth of God's Word. It contains over forty object lessons, each with teaching tips and related Bible passages.

The Youth Worker's Emergency Manual contains tons of great ideas, activities, games and Bible studies that you can use with just minutes' notice! Special articles on how to avoid emergencies and how to create a "prop box" help youth workers run their ministries with professionalism.

101 Outrageous Things to Do with a Video Camera gives offbeat, fun and easy ideas for using this medium with your youth group.

Magnetic Flyers, The Youth Worker's Clip Art, The Youth Worker's Son of Clip Art Book, I Was a Teenage Clip Art Book and ***The Bible Visual Resource Book*** contain illustrations for you to clip out and arrange to create mailers, posters, flyers, calendars, teaching aids and more.

Skitsophrenia is full of skits that teach Bible truths in an entertaining way. It also has skits for announcing events during a worship service or youth group meeting, skits to use for evangelization and articles on the art of presenting skits and how they can be used to build up the Body of Christ.

*These resources are available from Gospel Light Publications or your local Christian supplier.